"Toor immerses the reader in the world of long-distance running, examining her bruised, muscular body, the contents of her closet, her pantry jammed with energy gels and protein bars, and her love life in the process of explaining what running means to her and describing the experiences the sport has given her."—Jenny Shank, *New West*

"Readers who have thought about taking up running but have kept putting it off will discover that Toor has deftly taken away all of their excuses, from 'I don't have time' to 'I'm too out of shape' to 'It'll hurt too much.' A book that will appeal equally to novices and experienced runners."—*Booklist*

"In an unconventional, inspirational, and loving account of running, really well done and funny as heck, Rachel Toor shows how this simple activity is so powerful that it sweeps us off our feet into friendships that endure. I'm a fan."—Bill Rodgers, four-time winner of both the Boston Marathon and the New York City Marathon

"*Personal Record* takes you on a grand tour of the running life, which goes from hobby to one of the purest forms that fanaticism in sport can take—ultramarathons. As any great running book deserves, Rachel Toor's writing is swift, disciplined, sinewy, and indomitably strong. It is also hilarious. The story she tells is a marvel."—Pat Conroy, author of *My Losing Season* and *The Prince of Tides*

"In this gem of a book, Rachel Toor shares her thoughts and emotions as she tiptoes, trots, and eventually races into the quirky world of running. Toor's journey is a personal adventure, intimate and sometimes confessional, and runners of all abilities will enjoy traveling along with her."—Don Kardong, former Olympic marathoner and *Runner's World* senior writer

"How do I love thee, running? Let Rachel Toor count the ways—over land, with her body, alongside horses, with her closest friends—the endless, wonderful ways."—Kathrine Switzer, first woman to run the Boston Marathon and author of *Marathon Woman*

"Rachel Toor makes me want to be a runner. . . . We can all find something inspiring in this book of stories about her running experiences."—Doris Anne Roop-Benner, *Story Circle Book Reviews*

"I couldn't put it down. It's insightful, funny, and passionately real and personal."—Bernd Heinrich, author of *Why We Run: A Natural History*

"Rachel Toor is very brave, as a runner and as a writer. She sees things down at the cellular level and doesn't hesitate to tell you Difficult Truths. And, if it weren't for the fact that she confesses to breaking down and crying every so often, you might even think it was easy."—John L. Parker, author of *Once a Runner* and *Again to Carthage*

"If you believe that there are 60 seconds in the unforgiving minute, then believe me as much as you do your stopwatch when I say, you'll enjoy Rachel's story as much as you do a perfectly paced tempo run."—Roy Benson, author of *Coach Benson's Secret Workouts* and senior writer for *Running Times*

UNIVERSITY OF NEBRASKA PRESS: LINCOLN AND LONDON

PersonalRecord

A Love Affair with Running

Rachel Toor

Acknowledgment for previously
published work appears on p. 163,
which constitutes an extension of
the copyright page.

*Library of Congress
Cataloging-in-Publication Data*

Toor, Rachel.
Personal record : a love affair with
running / Rachel Toor.
p. cm.
ISBN 978-0-8032-6033-7
(cloth : alk. paper)
ISBN 978-0-8032-3426-0
(paper : alk. paper)
1. Marathon running.
2. Women runners.
3. Marathon running—Training.
I. Title.
GV1065.T66 2008
796.42'5—dc22   2008005352

Set in Minion by Kim Essman.
Designed by Ashley Muehlbauer.

For my brother, Mark

A personal record or, more commonly, a PR
is a runner's best time at a given distance.

Contents

Toeing the Line

I like to call it "The Oprah Effect."

Oprah said to us: *If I can do it, anyone can.* She had excellent professional trainers, and she did it surrounded by a coterie of helpers. But even the richest woman in the world couldn't pay someone to run a marathon for her. Oprah Winfrey had to take every step of the 1995 Marine Corps Marathon on her own. She finished in 4:29. This feat, heroic in its way, spawned a cottage industry of silly tee-shirts that said "I beat Oprah." But Oprah encouraged scores—hundreds, thousands—of middle-aged women, who looked in the mirror and did not see the whippet-thin shape of a distance runner, to hit the roads and start training for a 26.2 miler. Oprah inspired a bunch of swaggering men to want to go out and beat her time. Al Gore ran the same race two years later. He finished in 4:58.

Anyone can do it. It's all in the preparation. If you train properly, you should be able to hit your marathon goal—plus or minus five minutes—on race day without a problem. But that doesn't mean it isn't hard, or that 26.2 miles isn't a long darned way to go. If you don't train well, you may still finish, but it won't be pretty. Or fun. After crossing the line at the New York City Marathon, squeaking by in less than a minute under three hours, a ragged Lance Armstrong said the marathon was "without a doubt the hardest physical thing I have ever done."

Some run a marathon to cross it off their life checklist. For others, marathoning becomes an obsession, a habit of mind and body. For me, starting to run was not about losing weight or getting healthy. I began in order not be excluded; I ran so that I wouldn't be left behind. I've never been much of a joiner, but when I found something I loved doing—and realized that there were other people who shared my enthusiasm—I joined a running club. There are all kinds of different subcultures: gardeners, fly fishers, philatelists, economists, collectors of pig figurines. These are often solitary pursuits, but when clusters of zealots find ways of coming together—Internet chat groups, conventions, races—we turn into a herd, a pack. We recognize ourselves in each other.

By becoming a runner, I was welcomed by strangers as a comrade, and I gained, as my legs got stronger and my lung capacity increased, an increased and more complex capacity for friendship, especially with men. I have always had a handful of women I hold close—whose intense friendships I rely on, where we sustain and support each other. Through running I learned not to be one of the boys, but to be myself, a woman among men. I'm not a small talker. I tend to talk about big things, or speak not at all. Running gave me a lingua franca, a common language to share with new acquaintances.

This book is about how I evolved from a bookish egghead who ran only to catch a bus to a runner of ultramarathons. (Ultras are defined as any race longer than the marathon distance of 26.2 miles.) It was a pretty straightforward process and not that unusual: First I got my butt out the door and jogged for a while. I entered some shorter races, and then some longer ones. Then I just kept going. Once I'd done a handful of marathons, I started hanging around with a bunch of guys who used 26.2 milers as training runs for ultras, and poof: I was an ultrarunner. Bothered by the fact that running is a narcissistic activity—it's all about me, me, me—I got to a point where I wanted to shift the focus from myself. I found ways—pacing, coaching, helping others achieve their goals—to share my fervor that provides rewards beyond anything I could ever have imagined.

While I do not believe that there is such a thing as a runner's worldview—there are, I would argue, as many ways of thinking and feeling about running as there are runners—we do share certain things. Watching a big marathon is a remarkable experience. Depending on your vantage, you can spot individual runners, sure, but you also see the way in which we all come together as an organism, moving in unison, sharing a common goal. Here, in chapters that alternate with my personal record of becoming a runner, are meditations, examinations, and celebrations of the nuts of bolts of how we each hook into the pack. I look at and think about various aspects and accoutrements of a runner's life: clothes, food, races, racing, injuries, my watch (I love my watch; you will learn how much I love my watch). The things we all share; the things we all have.

I wanted the structure of this book to suggest the shape of a marathon. The way the early miles tick by, quick and light. How the middle part can get slow and hard. Like most difficult activities—writing books, learning to play an instrument, building a relationship—there's a pace. The middle portion is always tough: the transition of moving from something that seems easy at the start to an endeavor that becomes so hard it requires enormous will—in addition to strength—is challenging. It helps to have other people along. At a certain point, it becomes clear that you will make it, though, in a marathon, the last two-tenths of a mile are not trivial.

Running is the act of catching yourself before you fall. It is about keeping yourself upright as you move forward. The faster you go, the more there is at stake. You strike a balance between how hard you can push yourself and still remain in control. You straddle the line between fearless and reckless. At times, even if you are doing everything right, you fall.

During long races, you think about something for a while—sometimes it's a passing thought or random insight, other times an attempt to work out problems—and then you move on. The thinking is not entirely linear. After a while, you accept this. After a while, you settle in. And then, the mind goes its own way—slowing down, wandering more freely, giving itself over to the body, and finally, ultimately, to the heart.

PERSONAL RECORD

The Body

The feet are Gorgons. A look could turn you to stone. Rarely are there ten toenails. Often at least one nail is purple or black, so battered and bruised, the supply of blood cut off by built-up blisters, that it will, having wiggled too long like a loose tooth, come off in a sock.

The bottom of the right pinky toe is calloused to a sharp edge. It could cut you, if you grabbed it wrong. The top of the second toe on the left foot is scaled and horny, like a desert-dweller; the knuckle of the right middle toe hammers downward. The feet are white, even in summer. The feet are best unseen.

The lower legs are often mottled green and blue with bruises, scratched from shrubby branches. The knees have been skinned. They are mapped and patterned with scabs from falls onto rocks, and sliding crashes with trails. The scabs have, over the years, hardened into scars. There are big white divots on the right knee—one just above the jutting of the fibular head, the other on the far side of the bony cap. A sharp white line runs north from the bulging vein that traverses the left knee. There are more such lines, a map of veins and scars. They point nowhere. Go nowhere.

When the thighs are flexed, you can see the sartorius, the long muscle of sitting with crossed legs, the tailor's pose. Two discrete chunks of the quadriceps, unfeminine and bulky, bulge. The adductors—the *No!* muscles used to keep away the prying hands of high school boys—pop into view. From behind: the distinct bellies of the gastroc—the gastrocnemius muscle, the calf. It has been chiseled by the miles. Hamstrings are taut as violin catgut. The butt is hard, solid, though lower—try not to look—it is pocked with humanity.

The legs are bowed, a cause of teenage angst, a reason not to wear short skirts or skinny jeans. The legs are bowed, but now they are strong. Short skirts, short shorts, skinny jeans—there is no longer a reason to try to hide flaws. These legs are what they are. Bowed. Bruised. Scarred. Strong.

You could hurt yourself on the iliac crests. Or use them as handles. Do not use them as handles unless you mean business. The libido works like a muscle. With disuse, it atrophies. But exercised regularly, it calls for attention. Everything, it seems, acts together.

The gut is temperamental. It needs to be filled. It wants what it wants; it retains veto power.

There isn't much of a waist, no padding on the hips. The obliques come down at ropy angles from below the ribs, which are too visible (not fetching, to be seen with arms outstretched; reaching for the sky should be done in a shirt). There is no six pack; this is no partier's physique. The abs—the muscles of pelvic tilt, of sexual thrust—are not defined. The body is ungenerous, unyielding. There's little excess.

The breasts, however, are superfluous. Intense physical exercise and the concomitant lack of body fat suppress, in prepubescent girls, the production of estrogen. When the activity—gymnastics, say—stops, menstruation starts, finally, and cramps curse each month. Breasts spring unbidden and disproportionately large. They add unuseful weight. The ribcage remains tiny—tits on a toothpick, rail with a rack—conspiring for years of tears while shopping for bras.

Bony shoulders, neck and back muscles that are always sore from holding it all together. Upper arms with ripples, like sand after the ocean has pounded in and away. Lower arms, veiny, like a young boy's or an old woman's. On the palm of each hand are small reminders of the many times chunks of skin have been sacrificed during falls. (The ring finger on the right hand is still askew from a back handspring gone awry in childhood.)

The skin is too exposed, showing signs of the elements, and of wear. There are thin lines, small creases, freckles, and sun stains. For four and a half decades this body has been out in the world. For fifteen years, it has been pounded and pushed, challenged and badgered. It continues to hold fast.

In bed a boyfriend once offered that I had the body of a Tyrannosaurus Rex. I asked for an explanation and he gave one: big, muscular legs; scrawny, good-for-nothing little upper body. I pointed out that this might not be the best thing to say to a naked woman who was, at least for the moment, lying beside him.

He couldn't imagine how his statement might give offense.

It's, you know, he said, a runner's body.

Reasons Not to Run

In college I was a pretentious little intellectual. I wielded my mind with brute force, inflicting my opinions and ideas with speed and dexterity, bruising those who got in my way, but inhabiting my body only incidentally. Fortunate genetics, the metabolizing effects of an overachieving restlessness, or perhaps, simply, the will to power, kept me slender. I did not exercise. I never saw a reason to run. But many of my friends did.

Angular, blond Jacki, her face red from frequent washings with Clinique soap, would scrawl a note on my door: *Going out for a run. Back in twenty minutes. Dinner, then?* I would read some more pages of Henry James, James Joyce, George Eliot, and when she got back, we would go to the big freshman Commons dining hall to eat. She'd played field hockey in high school and was, it seemed, in the habit of running. I preferred my habit of reading too much.

Jacki read a lot as well, but mostly in Latin or Greek. She was a beautiful, sharp-edged girl from Philadelphia's Main Line, where, when she was at home for vacations, she would go to the Laura Ashley store with her mother and the two of them would shoplift, layering expensive dresses under baggy overalls. She dismissed most of our classmates as boring and drank her black coffee out of a glass. She made me feel like I could never keep up. Jacki did her running solo.

Junior year my roommate Val would come back, change into shorts and tee-shirt, and head out the dorm room door. She would meet up with others. They would go for—what? thirty minutes? forty? an hour?—and she would be showered and dressed before dinner. She did it—why? for exercise? relief? social contact?—and I never asked about it. I also never asked about her Chinese homework, and she rarely asked me about Milton. We did what we did. We were who we were.

Val was that special kind of Chinese American good girl. She was *guai*. She ran the way she did everything: deliberately, and with discipline and care. She played piano, didn't smoke, drank only occasionally and then temperately, got good grades and test scores, wrote thank you notes, kept her room clean, sewed tight loose buttons, spoke in Chinese to her grandma, circulated with ease and grace among different social groups, and she ran. She enacted the Greek ideals: mind and body, both sound; everything in moderation. Val worked hard. Jacki would have dismissed Val as boring, if she had bothered to talk to her. It took me some years to figure out that Val was a proper role model.

There's nothing like the laziness of a person who has gotten away too long with being smart. I coasted and did as little as possible. I drank some, tried the drugs that didn't scare me. A couple of times I went to the gym with friends, because they went. I slept with boys, slept with men, got good grades and praise from my professors, read books. I read lots of books; I lived in my brain.

After college, I settled in New York City and entered the workforce, toiling in the mind fields of scholarly publishing. Sarah worked in the production department and had to run two laps of Central Park every morning—6 miles—and on the weekends had to do three. She talked about it like that: she had to run. Olive-skinned and short-limbed, inclined to argue, subsisting on bagels and coffee, she was solid and striving to stave off fat. It worked. Sometimes she talked about how much she would run if she didn't *have* to. The answer seemed to be not much.

Andrew and I were introduced by a mutual friend when I moved to North Carolina. I was on the edge of thirty. He was a couple of years older, finishing his medical residency. Andrew had run track when he wasn't playing basketball in college. He'd run a 4:30 mile. I didn't know what that meant. What was the world record for the mile? Something like four minutes? Was an extra half minute a lot or a little? I had no gauge. When he told me that he'd been able to high jump six and a half feet I was more impressed; that I could visualize. Andrew is five-ten if you rub his hair with a balloon.

Most days before we could get together for dinner, Andrew would need to go for a run. This irritated me. I'd come home from work and be eager to get started on play. But instead, as in college, I'd be waiting around for someone to finish running before I could eat. It made me cranky. Andrew assured me that it was better for both of us if he got to run. He needed the exercise. I couldn't unpack this. Wanting to exercise—maybe. But needing? No.

Andrew and I went on vacation with Val and her then-boyfriend. We rented a big house on the Outer Banks of North Carolina. Above the door hung a sign that said, *Ancient Marnier*, a cause of delight and jokes: Was it the ancient mariner drunk on Grand Marnier? Really, really old liqueur? We spent mornings eating breakfast and days lying on the beach planning dinner. Then the three of them would go off for a late-afternoon jog. I stayed on the deck in my black bikini, eating Oreos and reading a nineteenth-century novel. I liked that Andrew was able to share this time my friends, but I didn't want to have anything to do with it.

I knew the litany, the multiplicity of reasons why people ran: that it was good for them, in some physical, emotional, or even soul-enhancing way; that energy and frustrations needed to be sizzled out, like the fat in bacon; that many people, and most women, were raised to be dissatisfied with their bodies, no matter what they looked like, and running was an efficient trade-off for brownies and ice cream; that we are social animals, some of us, and want time with others, even if it is at ungodly early hours of the morning and in weather that is not fit for

7

those who do not grow fur; that solitary time is a necessary condition for hard thinking; that competition is endemic to the human condition and harnessing it in innocuous ways and at appropriate venues will, perhaps, keep violence at bay.

I knew all of this, understood it in some intellectual, if not visceral way. I remained unconvinced. I did not want to run. Perhaps it was the tinge of fatalism that comes with reading too much existential philosophy, coupled with the callous, pig-headedness of healthy youth. More likely it was plain old laziness—not wanting to bother, not liking to sweat. I did not run because I did not have to.

Years later, thinking back on my beginnings, I see that while eventually I came to understand that running would be good for my body and for my mind, it took me longer to know what it would do for my heart. Not the knobby muscle that pumps blood through the body, the organ that keeps the physical self alive, but the notional place where feelings pool and clog and eventually spring free. What I didn't realize, when I first started lacing up my shoes, was that for me, running would be so much about love.

Running with another person is an intimate activity. Run with someone for long enough at a time and you will be stripped bare. Modesty falls away with the miles. The body—its functions, its excretions, its wants—cannot be ignored. The heavy breathing, the sweating, the soft talk that comes after exertion, the hours spent together—running with another person is an intimate activity. It's hard to keep the heart uninvolved.

The Routes

Horses are conservative. They don't like change; they cling to routine. You can be riding along the same trail you ride every day, and if there's a tree branch down or a rock out of place, it can be as if a bomb had gone off. Horses are reassured by monotony.

It's the idea behind chain restaurants—the familiarity of the menu, the expectations that are rarely challenged. You know what you're going to get before you even order. A Big Mac tastes the same in New York City as it does in Wallace, Idaho. We like this. It comforts us.

There is a solace in sameness. Running an identical route each day can be an affirmation, a pledge, a prayer.

There are loops where, no matter which way you go, you start out downhill. It doesn't take long to realize that means that finishing is always up. It is like this if you run around the golf course at Duke University. There were days when the thought of having to climb that last hill was enough to keep me from my running shoes. But after the first dozen times, the topography became familiar. I knew what to expect and the knowing made it easier. The rewards of downhill stretches, the places that always felt a little warmer, sheltered spots where the light changed—these were the things I looked forward to.

When starting out on a loop from my home in Durham, I knew that in the winter I would be cold until I got to the house with the alarm system sign in the front yard. It would take until the first uphill after the corner for my body to loosen, my legs to move more fluidly. When I saw the tree that had been uprooted by a hurricane, I knew that I was nearly back.

In Montana, I lived in an apartment in downtown Missoula. If I was tired, I could run on the city streets or on the path along the river. On energetic days, I could jog ten minutes to campus and then go up two thousand feet in less than 2 miles.

We look for markers. Sometimes we name them: "The Shut-in Simulator," "The Easy Way In," "The Three Larches Trail," "The Tree of Death." We need these monikers when we are running in groups and are trying to decide routes and distances. But when we run by ourselves, we make up names that we rarely, if ever, speak aloud. They are less clever, often, less elegant. "Where the trail narrows and the light barely gets through and the footing is soft and covered with pine needles" is one of my favorite places. I couldn't tell you more specifically where it is.

There are people who can run a course once and give you a topographical and geographical description as good as any military intelligence could muster. They will notice the inclines, be able to estimate the grades, and point out interesting features along the way. They will see things, discern things, remember things. These are good people to have around. Me, I notice almost nothing. But I have a lot of endurance.

Knowing that you are able to run for two, three, or four hours provides an opportunity to explore. There is no better way to discover a new city, a new place, than by running. Getting lost is okay, as long as you have water enough and stamina. Getting lost is a good way to find things.

There are the everyday, bread-and-butter routes—the subsistence loops. There are the places we visit only in groups, and those we share with no one. There are the special occasion runs—taking the Smoke

Jumper Trail up the side of Mount Sentinel and coming down the face; the 16 miles up Stuart Peak, where even in the summer, there will be crusted snow.

And there are the routes—the loop around the Duke golf course— that remind us of where and how we started. When we run them, we are transported back to our beginnings, to the time before we could really run.

One Runner's Beginnings

Andrew and I were introduced. We dated. Every week or so I'd threaten to break up with him. We moved in together. There were struggles over the toilet seat (*down*—it belongs down) and the kitchen cabinets (*closed*—they should be closed) and the dishes in the sink (*piled up*—they should *not* be piled up in the sink). But we never argued about Hannah, my dog.

Andrew started taking Hannah along on his runs. She would greet him at the end of the day with yelps and circle dances, and then wait, coiled for action, while he put on his compression shorts and pulled up his white basketball socks to just under his knees. Finally, they'd tear out the door. Some portion of an hour later, they would return home spent and content.

I grew jealous of their time together, and began to feel left out. First, because I was me, I made snarky comments. Then, after being encouraged by Andrew—he was always encouraging, always positive—to join them, I said, with a sneer, "Okay." We went to the trail that loops around Duke's golf course, 3 miles, all hills, woody and lush.

I said, "Okay, let's go," and took off, leaving Andrew in my wake. When he caught up, he suggested that the first mistake many new runners make is to start out too fast. You hurt early and decide that running isn't fun and never do it again.

"I'll set the pace," he said. "Just stay with me."

I complained that the pace he set was too slow.

"I can run faster than this, you know," I said, feeling that this was true, though not knowing it to be so.

"That's okay," he said. "Let's just start out slow."

Not five minutes later I was complaining that I was getting tired.

I did not notice the way the light came through the tall pines or hear the scuttering of birds on the ground. I did not smell the snakes.

"Slow down," he said. "Take it easy."

Hannah ran like a dog—she'd bolt ahead, and then charge back to us.

I told Andrew that he didn't have to wait for me, feeling guilty for holding him back. I knew this couldn't be much fun for him, knew that he wasn't getting any needed exercise. Plus, I was angry with him because I wasn't good at this. I hated doing things I wasn't good at. It is easier not to try new things. And it is unpleasant to have someone witness your struggle. Especially if you're an overachieving, high-strung, complaining whiner type.

"Just take it easy," he said.

He told me to walk up the steepest hills, and I argued—that wasn't running. He told me to relax on the downhills, not to try to make up speed or time. I wanted to blast down them.

I argued for the whole 3 miles, but when we stopped running, I apologized, astonished. I'd made it all the way around the loop.

For our next run we went to a more remote part of the Duke Forest where Andrew sometimes ran after work. He often had cuts and bruises from falling.

"How can you fall?" I wanted to know. "Grownups don't fall down."

Andrew did. A lot.

He worked late and ran at night, in the dark, on rocks and roots.

"How can you run at night? How do you see? How can you fall?

Don't you get hurt?" I questioned the reasonableness of this whole endeavor.

But then there we were, among loblolly pines and rhododendron, and we were running on a trail along a creek and it was beautiful and we saw deer and snakes and heard birds and the sound of our breathing and our footfalls. And then it began to rain. And I began to complain. We were approaching a hill, a big one. I was at once miserable.

"Tell me about schizophrenia," I barked out. Andrew did. He engaged my mind and I forgot about my body and before I knew it we had crested the hill and were almost back to the car.

It's elemental, running. It's not like doing classical philology or non-linear dynamics. You don't need to learn two dead languages and read the corpus of ancient literature before you can start to engage; you don't have to have calculus and physics under your belt and be able to think in seventeen dimensions. You just start with one foot and the other follows, because if it doesn't, you will fall. Little kids and animals know this.

I wanted Andrew to advise me on technique, to coach me, but he was a good teacher and knew that first you have to get someone started, and then you refine.

I was impatient and wouldn't stand for good teaching. "Tell me what I'm doing wrong," I'd demand, breathless. He would relent and give me bits and pieces: Don't clench your fists. If you want to increase your speed, shorten your stride. Going up a hill, take little steps. Going downhill, don't brace against it—just flow. He ran slightly behind me, making me feel that I was leading, that I was the stronger runner. He made me believe I could do it.

"Take it easy," he said.

"Breathe. Don't run so fast you can't talk."

We talked a lot, Andrew and I. He always had stories about family and friends, collections of antics from college and medical school, and explanations of the work of neurotransmitters or the various types of edible fungi. Once, we set out for a run, and I was cold. I'd underdressed and spent the first few minutes chanting, "I'm cold I'm cold I'm cold." That launched Andrew into a rhapsody on thermal equilibration—the physiology of the body's response to external temperatures. Andrew had been a lackluster high school student (though good enough to get into one of the nation's top colleges), but he had a restless curiosity and learned without forgetting anything that captured his attention.

Because we were human, and because we were in a relationship, we also had to have Talks, those terrible relationship talks with long silences and squinty eyes. Whenever we needed one of those sessions, we'd go out for a run. I learned that you can run a whole lot faster if you're pissed off or frustrated. We'd come home talked out, sweaty, having worked through whatever it was that needed working. I'd be exhausted. Andrew and Hannah never even seemed tired.

I began to look forward to running, going more frequently, and longer, just me and Hannah. In the heat of the North Carolina summer, she learned to stop to drink at streams. I asked her to lie down in them—to get her chest wet, to cool herself. She always did as I asked. She loved this new part of daily life. When she saw me get out my running shoes, she'd circle and wag, run to the door, to me, to the door. Her enthusiasm buoyed me.

One day I saw a sign on Duke's campus advertising a 5K race. "How long is 5K?" I asked Andrew. He told me it was a smidge over 3 miles, just about the distance of the golf course loop, which I was now able to run twice and no longer had to walk the hills. I signed up for the race.

I wasn't used to pushing myself, hadn't ever tried to run faster. I did that day, caught up in the pack of runners. What I wanted was the shirt. I got the shirt just for entering, before the race even started, but I also got something else: Among the thirty- to thirty-four-year-old women, I was the third-place finisher. I got a medal, heavy, silly, on a red, white, and blue ribbon. A medal and a shirt. I liked the idea of a material marker of where I've been and what I've done. Even now, years later, I still do.

The Closet

5

At a certain point, you have to get rid of them. There are always too many. They take up space. You can't keep them straight, even if you have learned to mark them, to inscribe the date of purchase in the footbed.

There are the current shoes—the ones you use every day. But you don't want to run in the same shoes every day. That's the way to court overuse injuries. So you keep at least two pairs in rotation. Crowding them are shoes that may be nearing the end of their running lives but are still good for rainy or muddy days.

Usually, as soon as you find your perfect shoe, they stop making them or change the design. So you learn to buy more than one pair if you find a model you like. These you store in boxes, stuffed with paper and the smell of newness.

There are trail shoes, at various points of the life cycle. The brand-new ones you won at a race; the old, almost-but-not-quite-ready-to-be-retired ones you love. The Gore-Tex–raincoated shoes for the snow. The ones you leave the Yaktrax on—like chains for snow tires—for icy days. There are racing shoes, light and fast. The special ones you save for marathons. The duds. A new brand you tried but didn't like. Ones that were given to you to test. Those from a sponsor that you refuse to wear because when you did, you got injured. And finally, the retired: shoes with too many miles to run in but still useful for mowing the lawn, riding a horse, or hiking with normal people.

The sock drawer is stuffed and hard to open. The vagaries of the dryer have taken its toll, and many are widowed, mateless. Still, you keep them. For winter you have smart and sassy wool pairs that reach up over ankles and snuggle inside tights. You have a variety of colors and weights, some thick, for the days when you are afraid that your little piggies will freeze; some thinner, for the shoes that are just a little too tight.

You have racing socks for marathons and racing socks for long trail runs. They are the same brand, double-layered to prevent blisters, but the trail socks are so stained with dirt it would be embarrassing to wear them on the roads. At a trail race, it's okay that your white socks are closer to dun. Trail running embraces the earth.

You still have some old cotton socks. You know that you shouldn't wear these—they will surely give you blisters if you sweat even a little. But still, you keep them. Just as you keep the freebies, emblazoned with brand names. Just as you keep the ones with holes and those whose elastic has lost verve.

Occasionally, you will purge the sock drawer. But like the miracle of the loaves and the fishes, there always seems to be more.

The bra drawer is less diverse. It consists largely of the Champion Action Shape for Large-Breasted Women in a variety of colors and states of being. Some are tattered and sheer from use. Others are crisp and unfaded. All clasp in the back, with the standard hooks and eyes of civilian bras. All are size 32D. There are some unworn over-the-head types. You have spent too much time wrestling with these—getting all tangled up in boobs, nearly tearing a rotator cuff trying to get them off—that you will not even try to put them on. They line the bottom of the bra drawer.

Shorts. Black, lots of black, in short, very short, and too long and baggy. Most are in men's sizes, where the lack of a waist is expected and accounted for; a few are women's. These don't fit as well. Some have pockets where you can store up to five gel packs, a fistful of dollars, and a car key. There are the prized yellow shorts with the familiar Boston unicorn. There are light blue ones with a waistband so loose that they threaten indecency with each outing. There are shorts for running fast and shorts for running slow. Slow shorts are longer, heavier, and baggier. Some are even cotton.

Then there is the skirt. It is for running. It looks hot on; it's cool to wear. There are panties sewn into it, as with running shorts, but it's not a skort. It's not a tennis skirt. It is for running. It makes you faster, especially at long, rough and tough, trail races. It is good to beat men when you are wearing a skirt.

About a dozen pair of black tights are crammed together. They range from nearly stocking-thin to padded. Some have reflective markings on them; some used to. Some zip up the back of the leg, some the side. Some do not zip at all. There are the tights and there are the looses. The looses are either man-sized, or cut not to cling. There are lots of holes. Just because it's cold enough outside to wear tights doesn't mean you don't fall.

Three drawers of shirts. The heavy, winter wear: zippered turtle-necks, fleece shirts, some with flaps that pull down and fold over like built-in mittens, some with holes for thumbs to poke out, to hold down the long sleeves that cover fingers. Hoodies that fit close to the body; capilene that wicks away sweat. Big old college sweatshirts for cold, slow days.

"Long-sleeved technical shirt" has become a clarion call for mara-thoners. Give the runners something they can use, goes the thinking. So, piles of shirts from races, silk-screened designs on synthetic ma-terials. Solid colors, lots of blacks and reds. Too much white. There are short-sleeved sisters to these synthetic creatures. And there are singlets. They look good on almost no one, except men with too much musculature to be serious runners. They go unworn. In the heat, the old, tattered, ripped, cut, homespun versions are more comfortable and feel, if not look, better.

And then, the many cotton race tees. Most come in sizes that are huge or very huge and are good only for sleeping. Rare races—those that are big and short—will have children's sizes. These fit small adults. Only a few—with good designs and in interesting colors—are worthy of street wear. Sometimes you can buy cute women's fit versions. Sometimes it is worth it. What makes for a good shirt is as consistent as what makes for a good haircut: It matters more to you than to anyone else, and it just has to feel right. Race directors will tell you that people almost never agree on shirts—some that many people love, just as many people hate. Pity the race directors.

There are jackets of varying weights, from anorexic Tyvek—little more than wrapping paper—to wind cheaters, rain busters, hooded anoraks, and Gore-Tex armor. If you are weather-averse, it is important to have the right clothes. The best of these combine function and bragging rights: a handsome and warm jacket that announces, discretely over the breast, "Lost Soul Ultra 50K" in colorful embroidery; a black polar fleece pullover proclaiming "Black Mountain Marathon."

At the bottom of the closet are strays: gaiters, like old-fashioned spats that fit over the shoe, to keep stones and dirt at bay; a variety of knee braces, with thick straps to hold the patella in place; ace bandages; sample packets of potions that heat or cool; blister-repair kits; a rolling pin–like utensil to attenuate stiff tendons; gear bags; goodie bags given out at races that convert into stringy backpacks. There are gloves, hats, neck gaiters for the cold; bandanas and baseball caps for the heat. There are water-bottle carriers, both for the waist and handheld; a Camelbak, its water bladder missing.

It doesn't take much to run—the essentials, for me, are good shoes and a supportive bra. But somehow, stuff accumulates. You get the things that make your life easier. Like can openers. Or a wireless router. Or the latest, greatest gear.

It's not only a result of the materialism that some of us can't resist—the desire to have. It's something else. It's about the fetishism that goes with any kind of zeal. These many things are a part of me. These shorts, this tee-shirt that can no longer be laundered without risk of disintegration, this special pair of socks—these are my runner totems.

The Coach

6

When I met him, Peter Klopfer was in his late sixties, with the field-darkened physique of a laborer and the clichéd hoary beard of an older professor. We talked about running; Peter, a veteran coach as well as a scientist, seemed interested in helping me get better, in indulging me in this experiment. A little unexpectedly, he asked if I rode horses. I had, as a kid, and told him that I was hoping to get started again. He rubbed his hands together and said, "I've got a little gray Arabian who's eager to meet you." And then he told me about the sport of Ride and Tie, a race where two people shared one horse to cover 30 or 40 miles of trail. I was intrigued.

I started spending time with Peter and his wife, Martha, at their farm, just outside of Durham. There were always other people there; graduate students, former and current; friends, many of them. You never knew who you were going to meet in the Klopfer's kitchen, but you could bet it would be someone interesting.

Audrey was there frequently, since she boarded her horse with them in exchange for her veterinary services. She was a few years younger than I, large-boned, quick to laugh, not long out of vet school, and an excellent athlete. We started riding together, big Audrey on her little horse Raj, little me on bigger Riesling. The Klopfers, oenophiles whose basement was lined with dusty, aging bottles, named their horses after wines.

As easy and as casual as Andrew was about running, Peter was just as rigid and systematic. He insisted that I keep a log, recording each day's mileage, the shoes I wore, the weather, and how I felt. That way, the scientist said, I would have data and could track patterns, could trace back things that led to injury or improved performance.

"Drink," he'd say, on a run, thrusting a bottle at me.

"I'm not thirsty," I'd counter.

"It has nothing to do with thirst," he'd say. "You need to drink before you think you need to." He would talk about electrolyte mixes needing to be isotonic, unless you required more salt and then they should be hypertonic. He referred to the surfaces we ran on as substrates.

If I started to develop an injury—if my calf felt tight, if there was pain on the side of my knee—he would be prescriptive and emphatic: ice every hour for twenty minutes. Or, run in the pool.

"But Peter," I'd say, "I work. I can't do that. Where am I supposed to get ice in the middle of the day? I don't have access to a pool." It didn't seem to matter that the world I lived in didn't match up with his worldview of putting running first, or that I had neither the time, the equipment, nor the money always to follow his suggestions. He knew the right things to do, and that was what he advised. He didn't like to tweak to fit the less than ideal.

I tried to do what Peter said. I trusted and respected him and appreciated the seriousness with which he approached his coaching. We would meet at the track, and only after we'd warmed up and done some strides on the infield would he tell me the workout. He would determine the distance, the number of repeats, the time in which to do them, and the amount of rest. I had to think about my training not at all; Peter did it for me. He'd watch me run and warn against stargazing—looking up instead of dead ahead; he'd remind me to swing my arms, to relax my shoulders and jaw. He gave me tips on hydration and nutrition and prescribed exercises for me to do at home. (Confession: I didn't do them.)

On the weekends, we would all do long runs together—Peter, Martha, me, Audrey, sometimes others. Occasionally we'd join a group that ran in the Duke Forest on Sunday mornings—many of them academics, some of them long-time friends of the Klopfers—but mostly we ran from the farm. Peter and I had fun and wide-ranging discussions. I responded as a student, pelting him with questions that could provoke dissertation-length answers that would cover miles. And not just about running. From Peter I learned about science, art, and even literature. A passionate opera fan, he tried, unsuccessfully, to convert me. He was quick to loan out possessions, to share ideas and food, and to bring people into his life.

I was grateful for Peter's friendship and coaching, but sometimes I bridled at his unyielding manner. During the years when I first started running, I'd have Peter coach me and then I would drift away. He would offer advice only when asked, though that did not mean he was good at concealing his opinions. If I showed up for a run in March, when the weather had softened enough that I felt comfortable wearing shorts, he would look at my pale legs and say, "Pushing the season, I see."

Peter, as generous a person as I've ever met, was stingy with praise. If he thought I'd run a good race—I always reported to him on my races and often read him the mile splits off my watch—I would find out only secondhand. Martha or Audrey would tell me that Peter had been pleased by my performance. His direct response was to point out the ways I could improve. Nothing was ever good enough, it seemed.

This style, I've learned, is a typical coaching approach. Many of my male friends recount stories of coaches that sound to me nothing less than sadistic. Pat Conroy's beautiful memoir about playing basketball at the Citadel, *My Losing Season*, is, in part, a profile of a clearly troubled man, his coach. But when I gave the book to a friend who had been a high school athletic superstar, he shrugged and said, That's what coaching is like. They tell you that you suck, and you work harder to prove them wrong.

Did I want Peter's approval because I trusted and valued his opinion, or because he withheld it? The combination of my need for praise and his inability to give it was volatile. He never told me that I sucked, but neither did I feel that I was ever good enough. Because I had no teammates, I had nothing to compare his treatment of me to, though he spoke in glowing terms of nearly everyone he knew. Peter had the rare ability to distill the nugget of whatever made a person most appealing to him and to ignore all else. If someone was arrogant, narcissistic, mean, or even stupid, it would matter to Peter only that he was an excellent runner, a terrific writer, a talented musician, or a serious scientist. He took from people the best of what they had to give, and ignored everything else. It is one of his most sterling qualities.

I suppose that the art of coaching is finding the particular ways to motivate each individual, and sussing out what kind of feedback will make her excel. It's not unlike editing—balancing the praise with the criticism. I didn't trust unalloyed admiration; I knew that wasn't going to make me better. But neither did the withholding sit well with me. So I would have him coach me for a while, would follow his program, and then I'd get disgusted and "fire" him. I'd come crawling back when I was getting ready for a race I cared about, when I got injured, or when I felt, for whatever reason, I needed him. He never took it personally when I bolted and welcomed me back each time without comment.

I have always been a good student, a type A cliché. If I was going to do something, I was going to be good at it. Peter was what I needed to become the only kind of runner I thought I was ever going to be. I was never going to jog for my health. I didn't care all that much about my health, having always been healthy. If I needed at some point to lose weight, there were easier ways to do it—starvation, say. No, with running as with all else, I wanted to be good.

The Magazine Rack

7

The essence of magazines is niche-ness. Each subculture has its own argot, its celebrities and scandals, its greatest hits. Each subculture has its bards and beacons of inspiration. Each subculture has its publications. After I'd been running for a while, I started to read the magazines.

The monthly articles on how to lower your 5K PR, how to eat more and weigh less, and how to figure out your tempo run pace were a revelation to me. (What was a tempo run?) On some level, I knew about the gravity with which some people approached running. But I didn't know there were quite so many of these folks. And so many rules and pieces of advice.

Everyone, it seemed, knew the 10 percent rule. Everyone except me. Apparently, you didn't increase your total weekly mileage by more than 10 percent. There were references to "Yasso 800s." I had no idea what these were, but when I read an article about them I was delighted by the magical quality. Bart Yasso, a longtime *Runner's World* guy, devised a workout that has kabbalistic overtones. Its beauty is in part its simplicity: you run repeats of 800 meters in the minutes and seconds of the hours and minutes of your goal marathon time. In other words, if you want to run a 3:30 marathon, you do your 800 meters in three and a half minutes.

Though I didn't pay much attention to the elite runners featured in the magazines, I liked the stories of regular folk—people whose lives were diverse and interesting and included, but were not limited to, running.

I skimmed the gear articles and couldn't make much of the shoe reviews. I wasn't sure how important things like the stability and weight of a shoe were to me. How much of a difference would a couple of ounces really make? Instead, I read to become versed in the language of running, its verbs made nouns (*splits, repeats*) its slang (*hammer, swag, bonk*), its terms of art, like *fartlek* and *rabbit.*

Most magazines recycle stories. The same questions come up over and over; small tweaks keep people reading. After a while, you get the main ideas. And then you see the tweaks. Can you run faster if you run less? If you weigh less? If you do most of your running on a treadmill? In the cold? On the beach? Are you less likely to be injured if you cross train? In some ways I read for information, but mostly I read for affirmation. I read to know that I wasn't alone.

Running has never felt like a sport to me, at least not the way team sports feel like sports. There, the goal is simple: to win. With running, the rewards are more complex, often more particular. The opponent can be a clock, a trail, or a distance. For most of us, winning is beside the point; that's often about who else shows up on any given day. So the running magazines have to be about more than just the winningest runners. And they are. If we want to read to feel part of a large community, *Runner's World* is the place to go. It shows off runners in all their glossy diversity, from the very fast to the Penguin, a regular guy who inspires the slow with his charming closing phrase, "Waddle on, friends." The hard core, those who want to get faster, read *Running Times.* When I subscribed, the tagline on the cover read, "For the Serious Runner." I loved this. Even if I wasn't fast, I was trying to be serious. And I wanted to get faster. I consumed each issue cover to cover. And I continued to read *Runner's World.* I saw the virtues of both magazines. I still do.

I began to look forward to the mail, if only to get the latest issues of my club newsletter and the regional running publications. Reading the race results was a way of keeping track of who had been where, who had done what: *Wow, look at Cathy's time! Wonder why Scott ran so slowly?* It was always a thrill to see my own name listed, and my times. I knew that other people noticed. It made me feel like a real runner.

Many of the running publications, especially the local and regional ones, feature pieces by people who don't think of themselves as writers. But something compels them to tell their tales, to share the things they've learned. Sometimes they do it in club newsletters, sometimes in e-mails and on list-servs. Sometimes they get published in *Ultrarunning* or *Marathon&Beyond*. Sometimes even in *Running Times* or *Runner's World*. The experience of doing something that feels epic often generates a need to figure out what it was about, what it meant, and then to share that. We humans think using language; we often decipher our lives by writing about them. I love that running can be a way for people to discover their writing chops.

Just as learning to run opened up a world for me, starting to write about running deepened my understanding and experience of that world. I have gotten to know other writers, some professional, some not, and have been invited as a journalist to run in the Himalayas, in Thailand, and in races across the country. I've made friends with people I've profiled, and I've profiled my friends.

My running and my writing have been intertwined. But the more I've shifted my focus to writing as a career, the more I've appreciated how, with running, the markers of performance are clear. The clock tells its own story. Races have their beginnings, middles, and ends. Unlike with writing, you know when you're finished, and when you've done a good job. You know if people are watching, and you know who you are competing against. William Styron apparently once said that the problem with Norman Mailer was that he saw writing as a track race. It's true that many writers are competitive. But who's to say where the finish line is, or even that we're all in the same race?

I do much of my writing on long runs, when I'm going slowly

enough to be able to think. If I'm trying to figure something out, I'll hold onto it until I'm able to put on my shoes and get out the door. I'll keep running until I have the answer it seems I need. Sometimes, when I'm racing, the thing that keeps my mind off the discomfort I am feeling is the story I will tell about it when I'm finished.

But, to tell you the shameless, needy truth, the best part of writing about running is when I go to a race, tell someone my name, and they say "Oh, I know you. I've read you." That never gets old.

Ride and Ties

8

We're sitting around the campsite the night before the thirtieth annual World Championship Ride and Tie. I'm talking to Warren Hellman, a San Francisco venture capitalist. Warren is cute, in a sixty-something Woody Allenish kind of way. He was a partner at Lehman Brothers when he was twenty-six years old and president not many years later. These days he buys and sells companies and does endurance sports. He's nursing a sore hamstring.

"How'd you get injured, Warren?"

"Yoga."

"Yoga?"

"I was sitting on the floor with my legs split," he says. "My yoga teacher commended me on my flexibility. I said, 'Oh yeah, watch this: I can get my chest to the floor.' Then, pop."

It's a competitive crowd I'm hanging out with, here in the mountains just north of Santa Cruz. We've come to race in a sport that has been described as what would happen if you took the Kentucky Derby and the Boston Marathon to Outward Bound. The people who are attracted to this unusual sport tend to be involved in equally unorthodox endeavors: ultramarathon running and endurance riding. Among us in camp are bankers, lawyers, doctors, artists, contractors, engineers, teachers, academics, loggers, small-business owners, large-business owners, veterinarians, accountants—fairly diverse, except that we are all white and most have enough disposable income to own and train horses.

It's a three-member team, two people and a horse. I start out running, you start out riding. You'll get to a predetermined spot and stop, tie the horse securely—but with a quick-release knot—to a tree, and continue running along the course. I will get to the horse, untie him, and then gallop to overtake you. At that point we will either do a "flying exchange," where I come up beside you, bail off the right—or more properly, the "off" side of the horse—while you mount from the other. Or we'll confer and decide that I will ride on ahead and tie some minutes up the trail. We will continue like this for the 30 or 40 miles of the race, leapfrogging all the way.

The potential for disaster is great: horses are competitive beings with big hearts. They will literally run themselves into the ground. The day before the race, a team of veterinarians goes over each horse. During the competition there are two to three "vet checks," where each animal is looked at for soundness, hydration, and signs of metabolic disorders. Horses are surprisingly delicate creatures. If anything is the slightest bit off, the horse will be taken out of the race. If a horse is pulled at a vet check, the other runner, the partner who rode in and ran out, may not find out about it for a while. So she just keeps running. If you're the one running, it can be, well, vexing.

Another challenging element is tying the horse. When you hitch a horse to a tree, the horse—a herd animal generally not used to standing quietly while all his friends go charging past—will turn himself around. If you pick a spot where there's trail on one side, but a drop-off on the other, you can't be sure that the horse will not fall. You have to scout out the whole circle around the tree. You have to tie your horse so that he will not block the trail and therefore the path of the other racers. But if you tie too far off the course, it's possible that your partner, especially later in the race when fatigue sets in, will miss the horse. That she will, in fact, run right past the horse. At this point, both people are running in front of where the horse has been tied. This is not good.

The Santa-bearded inventor of the sport of Ride and Tie has shot the starting gun (or, in later years, dropped a black hat to keep from spooking already-agitated horses) at almost every championship race for the last three decades. This year, again, Bud Johns drops his hat and the riders take off at a gallop. At the same time, the other halves of the teams start out running, mostly behind the horses and breathing in the dust kicked up by hundreds of hooves; less intrepid riders start out behind the pack but then go galloping past the runners, calling out, "on your left," or "passing on the right."

The trail funnels from the large meadow onto a steep, rocky dirt road. My partner this year, Mary, has done all of the championship races since the beginning of the sport. She is a strong runner and an excellent rider, with a good, sporty little horse.

Mary rides Albi about three-quarters of a mile up the road and then gets off and hands him to our waiting pit crew. For the first exchange, since the horses are usually so wired at the start, you are allowed a "hand tie." I come running up to where Wilma, Mary's sister, holds our little bay Arab, and I climb on. Around me, at various points on the trail, other competitors are getting on their horses, some of whom are spinning in circles around the folks holding them.

I'm on Albi, and before I can get my other foot in the stirrup, we're off. His ears are pricked forward and he's cantering up the trail. I'm able to rest a little from the climb but am still buzzed from race-start adrenaline. We pass runners. We pass riders. After a couple of minutes, we see Mary, running along. I call to her to let her know we're there and trot along beside her on the right. I hand her the reins and the tie rope, she takes them and I swing off the right (wrong) side of the horse. She's getting on the left (correct) side and takes off. That's the first of about thirty flying exchanges that we will do over this 31-mile course.

Back on my feet, I run easily, chatting occasionally with other runners. I know many of them, though I've only been competing for five
years and most of them have been at it for decades. They talk about the
Ride and Tie family. I'm afraid it's a little inbred at this point. There
have been a number of Ride and Tie relationships and marriages, and
some nasty Ride and Tie breakups as well. A couple of families have
three generations of Ride and Tiers.

I run for a little more than a mile and then spot Albi tied to a tree.
He has been looking for me. I get there, untie him, and before I am all
the way into the saddle, we are once again tearing down the trail. My
big fear is that I will make the classic mistake. You're not a real Ride
and Tier, they say, until you have run past your horse.

After about 12 miles of exchanging like this, every mile (or half
mile, depending on how steep or difficult the terrain is) with Mary
tying and me picking him up and then handing him off to her (some
teams have both people tying the horse, leapfrogging ahead of each
other), Mary gives Albi to me and tells me to ride him all the way into
the vet check.

During last year's championship race, I rode in and ran out of the
vet check. I kept running. I ran up a mountain. I started running down
the mountain. My partner finally caught me after around 7 miles. Turns
out our horse threw a shoe and had to have both back shoes replaced
by a slow-moving farrier not familiar with the logistics of the race and
the need for speedy work.

As I'm galloping into the vet check, volunteers ask for my number.
"Five," I shout. "Five coming in," I hear relayed back to the crew area.
By the time I get there, our pit crew is greeting me and taking the
horse away to be cooled off while he waits for Mary to run in and take
him through the check. (Teams must change riders at the checks.) As
soon as I'm off Albi, I'm running out again on Loop Two. My friend
Marnie, who has come down from Oakland to crew for us, is trotting
along with me.

"What do you want?" she asks. "Gatorade and a banana," I answer. We're running; I'm eating. She tells me there are six teams ahead of us.

After the start, things get pretty spread out. We've been running near a couple of teams, but it's hard to know how far from the front we are. Now I know. Loop Two has two huge climbs. I'm feeling pretty good. I've been running 50 to 60 miles a week but not riding very much. I don't own my own horse but still go out to the Klopfers periodically to ride.

I've been running for about nine minutes, a bit over a mile, when Mary comes riding up behind me. "He was down when I got in," she says. "Down" means that his pulse and respiration were at the numbers decided on by the vets before the race—recovered enough to be able to continue on.

While we're riding and tying, making our exchanges going up a 4-mile stretch that climbs about fourteen hundred feet, then descends again to sea level, after which there is another climb—and descent—of just over a thousand feet, we are keeping up with a solitary runner, Jeff, Warren's partner.

Jeff is a speedster, a strong, smooth runner who will end up doing at least three-quarters of the race on foot. Warren rides the hell out of his horse to keep up. Finally Warren catches Jeff out of the vet check, and the four of us are together on Loop Two. There are two more teams a bit behind us, and we don't know how far ahead the leaders are. Suddenly Jeff stops. He has a cramp in his hamstring. We pull ahead.

Into and out of the second vet check, we are in sixth place. The third and last loop is only 6½ miles. But the first three are straight up. It seems unlikely that our finish place will change on this loop. We are alone. Mary takes less care to make sure that Albi is tied securely, sometimes just tossing the tie rope over a branch. Each time I come running up to him he is facing me. After Mary leaves him, he watches her take off down the trail and then turns his body to look for me.

"Hey, Albi boy," I call out to him and he nickers back softly. He gets this sport. I've heard endurance riders say that they never really understood their horse until they did a Ride and Tie. We go through groves of redwoods; we turn corners and come out on spectacular vistas overlooking the Pacific. Parts of the trail are barren, with scrubby brush and shale; along the creeks, the foliage is lush.

We time our last exchange perfectly: I am running in fast; Mary is galloping to catch me just before the finish. The race isn't over until all three of us cross the line. It has taken just under four and a half hours to cover the 50 kilometers of the race.

We come in sixth overall, second woman/woman team. For our efforts, we get a lot of fluffing from other competitors, a fleece-lined vest donated by Patagonia, and a halter for the horse. It didn't used to be like this. There used to be money—cash prizes. Levi's ponied up the bucks when it first sponsored the race. Prize money was doubled if a winning team was wearing a piece of Levi's clothing. In some of the early photographs, you can see people running in their jeans—mostly cut off into shorts. In order to avoid leg chaffing during the ride, competitors would wear panty hose under their jeans shorts. In the early days, it was hard for the big men to find large enough hose. Eventually folks started getting creative and sewing Levi's patches onto their running tights or singlets.

I have now done six championships. At the first I partnered with a woman I didn't know, who, like me, was from the East Coast and who, like me, didn't have a horse. We both traveled to California to camp out with a group of strangers. We leased a horse from a woman who rode in a cowboy hat, tank top, and no bra. (She needed a bra.) At that first race I met the cast of characters I have reunited with for as many years as I have been able to make it back.

I have taken hot showers under circled stands of redwoods. I have eaten abalone, pounds of it, plucked from the Pacific by my fellow Ride and Tiers and grilled under the shade of ancient trees. I have brought Flutternutter sandwiches to the pre-race potluck and talked for hours about books while seated in collapsible chairs around fires or in fancy horse trailers outfitted like homes. I have walked around camp early in the morning promising to exchange a first-born child for a cup of coffee. I have danced late at night after the race, shaking the lactic acid from my booty and legs. I have learned, the hard way, to pitch my tent away from poison oak and stinging nettles. I have even, once, relaxed in a hot tub fashioned out of horse troughs, the water heated by a engine of a pickup truck.

I have won the woman/woman division of the race and the man/woman division as well. I have come in fourth overall—with a partner who had been planning to race with someone else on a horse who had been brought along only as company for a younger and fitter stablemate. I have saved the shirts, hats, horse halters, and buckles I have won. Each year I yearn to go back. Some years, I am able to make it.

9

Weekend Mornings

Sundays, 8 a.m., Duke Forest, Durham NC: Walter, Jim, Jim, Ole, Gordon, Paul, Scott, Steve, Gary, Charles, Carolyn, Glen, Owen, Jeff, Emil, Marvin, Mike, Cathy, Brian, Bob.

Saturdays, 8 a.m., Umstead Park, Raleigh NC: Scott, Steve, Steve, Stephen, Roger, Ralph, Lew, Chris, Ken, Jim, Paul.

Sundays, 8 a.m., Dean's house, Missoula MT: Dean, Joe, Jeff, Jeff, Eric, Greg, Kevin, David, Mo.

Weekdays, high noon, Teagle Hall, Ithaca NY: John, John, Boris, Bruce, Bob, Steve, Terry, Jeffrey, Lorrie.

Since I started running, my weekly long runs have been done in the company of bunches, mostly, of men.

One of the reasons I love running with men is that you can talk about nothing for hours. The same joke can be tortured and attenuated to within an inch of its life—and yet, on the twenty-third telling someone adds a tiny twist that continues to make it amusing. You can run with the same guys for years and never know the names of their wives, children, partners, or bosses. You may have only the sketchiest idea of what they do for work. You probably won't know where they grew up or went to college.

But you will know exactly which races they have coming up and what their PRS are. You will know about their injuries, the workings of their GI systems, and the new shoes and gear they've discovered. You will know some part of their essential selves.

Virginia Woolf wrote, "I often like women. I like their unconventionality. I like their completeness. I like their anonymity." What I like about men is their conventionality, their predictability; their inability not to rise to obvious bait; my ability, often, to finish their sentences. I like their lopsidedness, the urge not to integrate all parts of their lives. I like their egos—the chest-beating, the barbaric yawps sounded when they celebrate themselves. I like that they celebrate themselves.

You see all of this on weekly long runs. They are more than a training device. They are a way of life, a culture, a testosterone shower.

Over the years, no matter where my long runs have been, it's usually the same guys with different names. Sometimes they have the same names. What I can count on is that there will be camaraderie, competition, and easy banter. It's an intimate act, running together each week for some number of hours. Out in the woods or on the streets while the sun is still low, you have privileged time—time that most of us wouldn't set aside for a coffee klatch. Away from the exigencies of daily life, you are free not to think about them. And so, often, you don't.

There's usually a hierarchy. Since most people who train also race, everyone knows who's the fastest. You value him for that and give him a hard time, but also you wait, without comment, for those who are not as speedy. While there can be acting out—pushing the pace—the competition comes more from the mouth than from the legs and lungs. Doing the dozens, it's called in some places. Talking smack, in others. Feelings rarely get hurt. Feelings are beside the point.

Some are born leaders; some have leadership thrust upon them. Someone has to organize—to decide what time to leave and from where, which route to take, how long to go. Sometimes this is done by consensus; often the groups are led by someone who, in civilian life, has a management job. Other times there's a strong personality, a guy who says, *This is what I'm doing. Follow me if you want.* People usually want to follow a guy like that.

You can land in any city—and many towns—and find a bunch of guys who get together on a Saturday or a Sunday, early, regardless of weather. They will be named Ralph, Scott, Steve, Jim, Joe, Jeff, Dean, or Eric. They will be doctors, lawyers, professors, cabinet-makers, financial planners, lawn mowers, physical therapists, scientists, retailers, real estate agents, accountants, dentists, and the unemployed. If you're unlucky, there will be writers. Writers tend to talk a lot (and be unemployed). They may write about you. Watch out for writers.

There will be a host—someone who, by dint of personality more than official capacity, will welcome you and make you feel at home, ask you questions, and explain the route. He will give you the down-low on who the fast guys are, which are the interesting characters, whom to watch out for. There's usually someone to watch out for, if only because he stands too close when he speaks and tends to spit. Or he is reflexively lecherous. Or he is a writer.

Having a stranger drop into the group can alter the dynamics. Sometimes it's a welcome break, a new person to tease; sometimes language or content will be shifted down a gear, especially if the stranger is a woman. It's your job, as a strange woman, to assure the guys that they should be themselves. If you don't want to hear *your momma* cracks and potty humor, you should run somewhere else.

There are also, of course, groups of women running together. This is different. The conversations tend to have more substance; feelings get discussed, and the names of partners and children are known and remembered. I like to drop in on the girls from time to time, but, in truth, I am more comfortable with the guys. Gender being what it is—a spectrum—there are often women with the men, and men with the women, and men who are more like women, and women who are like me: more like men.

In fact, my closest women friends are runners. Val has continued to run the way she did in college—as a means to get a break, a method to stay healthy in mind and body. Sometimes when I am visiting with her we will go out for a run together, and then she'll turn around for home and I'll keep running. I like to go longer. We tend to hang around in our underwear after showering and continue the six conversations we started on the run.

I met Candace through our common connection to *Running Times*, and she fast became one of my closest friends. She has a grace and strength that I admire, a sense of humor that I love, and a brain that I cherish. She is my kite string. We rarely run together. Candace doesn't like to go with me because she thinks I'm faster and doesn't like the pressure to have to run harder to keep up; she doesn't like the guilt of feeling she's holding me back. Even though I tell her that I don't care how fast we run, I understand her reluctance. We talk about running, but we don't do it together. We don't need an excuse to spend two hours just talking; we don't have to run when we have cell phones.

Generally I don't talk on the phone with my running buddies. We use quick e-mails to arrange times and places, and then we meet up, at the trailhead, in the parking lot, at someone's house, and go. I can think of no better way to spend a weekend morning than making fart jokes and talking about races for two or three hours in the company of a bunch of guys named Jeff, Joe, Steve, Stephen, Scott, or Dean.

The First Marathon

10

We were finishing up an easy run on the golf course loop and had just turned onto the campus. Peter was headed toward the gym, and I was going back home. I was nervous, tentative. Finally, I asked it casually, as if I were wondering about what he was having for lunch, or if it was going to rain. I asked Peter if he thought I could ever do a marathon.

"Sure," he said, in a quiet tone. I caught a glint in his eye. "But," he warned, slowing just a little, "it's not worth it unless you can finish in under three and a half hours. Otherwise it's too hard on the body." At this point I'd been around enough other runners to know that Peter, while seldom wrong, was never in doubt about his positions. Maybe that was true; maybe not. "I'll write you a program," he said.

Audrey had done a marathon or two before, and was ready to try again. She'd been injured, and busy, but was getting fit. She and I trained together, doing long runs on Saturday mornings before riding in the afternoon. She rarely had the time to run with the group from Duke Forest, a bunch of guys I had begun meeting religiously every Sunday morning for 9 to 12 miles.

We decided on the Camp Lejeune Marathon, mostly because it was close. It was small, low-key, and on a marine base about two and a half hours away. Val was scheduled to visit that weekend. Andrew, now an ex but still a close friend, said he'd come along, too, so we decided to make a field trip out of it. Mike, also an ex-boyfriend, would have come along if he hadn't just busted his Achilles playing basketball with Andrew. We promised to call as soon as the race was over.

We got up early, drove to the base, and then spent a couple of hours pinning packets of gel to our shorts and listening to me whine. I was nervous. I was shooting, of course, for Peter's prescribed time of 3:30. Audrey had a friend visiting that weekend as well, a runner, who decided at the last minute that he didn't want to watch. So on the morning of the race, without having trained, he too entered the marathon. This made it harder for me to complain.

The course was a big flat square, windy and unadorned with civilian life. Val and Andrew drove around and planted themselves at numerous spots. They cheered for Audrey and her friend. They cheered—loudly— for me. They were among the few non-runners, non-marines on the course, so they cheered for everyone. They were such friendly oddities—an Asian American woman and a balding Jewish doctor—that after the race, marathoners came up to them and thanked them for the support.

I felt fine at first. At around mile 8, a woman handing out water said: "You're almost there." That made me mad. I knew it was not true. It didn't help. Why did she say that? What was she trying to do? The wind was blowing, and we were running into it. Everything looked the same. I was tired. When I saw Andrew and Val, they looked rested. They looked like they were having fun. I was not having fun. I was getting pissy.

We had planned to have Andrew run the last 6 miles with me. I thought that would make it easier. But when I got to mile 20 and there he was—I could see him from a distance, stretching like a seven-year-old ballerina, pulling his socks up to his knees—I knew that I wanted to be left alone. I ran past them. Andrew fell in beside me, and I barked at him to go away.

"Go away? I thought you wanted me to run in with you."

"Changed my mind. Go away."

"You don't want me to run with you?"

"No."

"Are you okay?"

"No. Go away." I used up energy I didn't have to make a shooing gesture with my hand.

"Are you sure?"

"Go. Away. Now."

Poor Andrew was 6 miles from the finish, from Val, from the car. He had no choice but to run in. He dropped back and stayed behind me, while I fumed and slogged and cursed my way to the end. I felt desiccated, dehydrated, dead.

When I crossed the finish line, I asked for IV fluids. My friend Luke, an anesthesiologist who sometimes ran with us in the Duke Forest Sunday group, had told me a story about going for a long run in the morning and giving himself an IV while he ironed a shirt to go out on a date that evening. It helped, he said. I wanted IV fluids, but they wouldn't give them to me without taking me to the hospital, and I knew that I didn't need to go to the hospital, unless it was to be treated for bad temper and embarrassment. I hadn't made my goal. I was afraid to go back and tell Peter my time. Audrey had run well, as had her friend who'd not trained at all. I felt like a failure and thought I would never do another marathon. Perhaps I would simply stop running.

After I'd eaten some food, apologized to my good, tolerant friends, and changed into clean, dry clothes, we went into the gym for the awards ceremony. I had placed in my age group. I got a shiny metal medal and a pen stand.

I learned later, when I showed up at the Duke Forest Sunday run with my head hung low and recited my disappointing finishing time, that I'd qualified for Boston.

I'd been told how to prepare for the marathon. Peter had been specific about my training. I had had to build up to at least 25 to 30 miles per week before he would even consider writing me a schedule. When he was convinced that my body was strong enough, he handed me a piece of graph paper with his sketchy scrawl on it. Each week was broken down by day, and each day had its own kind of run. Sundays were for long runs, building up by no more than 2 miles at a time (to a total weekly increase of no more than 10 percent). Peter was insistent on the 10 percent rule. "To do otherwise," he warned with the look of a finger-wagger, "would be to court injury."

I averted my eyes.

"New runners," he said, "usually want to do too much too soon. I worry not that you won't follow the program, but that you will exceed it. Do not exceed it."

The long runs should, he said, be LSD: Long Slow Distance. They should be run at a leisurely pace. They should be done in company, with interesting conversationalists and stops for fluids—both in and out.

Tuesdays were for track workouts. Running fast for short distances increases the body's ability to process lactic acid, builds up different muscles, and fine-tunes mechanical efficiency.

Thursdays were tempo runs: medium-length runs done at quicker-than-marathon pace.

In Peter's schedule, there were no rest days, no days completely off, but there were recovery days. Then you either ran slow and easy, or you did something else. Cycling was a good thing. As was running in the pool.

It was, I learned, a standard schedule. There are an abundance of programs that say essentially the same thing, and they can easily be found on the Internet and in running magazines. There are no tricks or shortcuts to marathon training. You just have to do the work.

And so I did.

Two weeks before the marathon, Peter told me "the hay is in the barn." Whatever training I did now would do me no good on race day; it takes fourteen days to see training effects, he said, so now what I had to do was rest.

Resting—tapering—was not so easy. I got crabby and restless, running much less than I had been, much less than I felt like. He told me to expect the irritability and that I might even gain a little weight. Expecting both helped me cope with neither.

It takes forty-eight to seventy-two hours to store food as glycogen in the muscles and the liver. So two to three days before the race, I was to eat carbohydrates. The night before, he said, I should not eat much. You want the food to pass through you before the race starts.

I was fully and well prepared for the marathon. Ready for it to be, as the clichés go, a 20-mile warm-up for a 6-mile race; to feel that the halfway point was at mile 20; to know that I would be excited at the start, tempted to go out too fast, and to expect to have to work hard to keep myself in check. Any minutes I gained in the beginning would not be banked but would be held against me like a grudge over the last few miles.

I went into the marathon knowing fully what to expect.

But no one told me what it would be like afterward.

I've since done enough marathons to warn first timers about the things that may surprise them.

I'd been told that I wouldn't sleep the night before. The excitement, anticipation, and pent-up energy from having tapered would make catching Zs about as likely as capturing a single electron. It was the night before the night before, in any case, that mattered most for a good performance.

But no one told me that, exhausted as I would be, not to expect to sleep the night after running a marathon. You lie in bed, worn out, feeling sore in muscles that you couldn't name or find on an anatomy chart, and cannot sleep. The body is a perverse joker.

You anticipate being depleted—which you are—and emaciated. Three to four hours is a long time to be running and a lot of calories to have burned. But no. You finish the race and walk around feeling fat. Bloated. Porked out. Your whole everything is swollen like a bruise.

And the yawning. There's constant yawning, as the body tries to recover some of that oxygen, tries to enrich the blood. You're tired, swollen, and yawning, but you can't sleep.

You may have gotten through the last few miles by fantasizing about cheeseburgers or pizza. You will have been told, no doubt, that eating some protein within thirty minutes of finishing is your window of opportunity to restock glycogen stores, to nourish that which held together your feeble self.

But you will have to force yourself to eat. It will not come easily. Eating becomes yet another trial. The guys who look forward to pounding beers at the end will likewise be disappointed.

What you will want most is the thing you should not do. You will want to submerge yourself in a hot bath and whimper. Go ahead, whimper. But if you must get in the tub, fill it with ice water. That is what your body needs.

A bone-deep weariness sets in and settles over you, like a heavy blanket. Shuck it off. It is better to spend time walking around, moving the lactic acid through the system, not allowing it to pool in spots that will be sore to the touch. It is better to do this, though it is more appealing to lie around and watch old episodes of *Melrose Place*.

The next day you may be surprised by how good you feel. Perhaps it wasn't that hard; perhaps all the training paid off. But again, the trickster grins. It's not the day after. It's the day after the day after. DOMS: Delayed Onset Muscle Soreness. That's when you'll be walking backward down stairs or off curbs because you can't bend your legs and expect your quads to come to your support. Not after what you've put them through.

The most surprising thing about doing a marathon is that when you're finished, you're likely never to want to run again. You certainly aren't going to go for another 26.2 miler.

It takes maybe a week.

The woulda, coulda, shouldas hit. I would have hit my goal if I hadn't gone out so fast, trained harder, hadn't eaten that Pop-Tart. I know I could have done better. I should have worn my lucky red undies.

And then, there you are, sending off a form and a check to enter another marathon.

11

Speed Goggles

There was a time in my hapless dating life when I told friends I was looking for a man who was STYF: Smarter, Taller, Younger, and Faster.

It didn't seem too demanding a list. But like many such lists, it was reductive and stupid and not so helpful. Smartness is a tricky category. I like to learn new things and tend to hang around people from whom I can glean knowledge. I need to be with someone whose mind zigs and zags in ways that enchant me, whether by listening to him talk about Penrose tiles or by watching him pack a moving truck. Likewise, I want someone who wants me because he likes the sounds my sentences make on those rare occasions when they sing. A man smart in exactly the right ways is hard to find, even though, according to some quick-to-e-mail readers of my columns, there are invertebrates smarter than me.

Taller isn't a tall order: I'm five-three. But like one of those yappy little dogs with a big dog personality, in my own eyes, I stand at least six feet. Some gentlemen prefer blondes; I go for tall men. There's no accounting for taste, and I won't make excuses for mine.

Younger—well, that gets easier by the minute. By the time this is published, I'll be practically older than dirt. Younger men are used to seeing strong women in positions of power. Show me a fellow who can articulate why he hates everything Hillary Clinton stands for but would never think to call her "opinionated" and that's a guy I'd like to date. When I get fired up about something, when my passions give voice to ideas, I don't want to hear that tired TV line, "Why don't you tell us how you really feel?" You might as well pat me on the head and coo, "Settle down there, little lady." Younger men tend not to say stupid shit like that.

Finally, I'm a runner. Not only that, I'm a snob, if being a snob means that I value excellence. One summer I basked in reflected glory by hanging out with Nate, a D-III runner, who won every trail race he went to. Nate was describing a girl he was interested in. I asked what compelled him about her. "She's really fast," he said, in as close to hushed reverence as a college boy can get.

Anything else?

Fast was enough, it seems. He explained: speed goggles. I've been around enough college students to know about beer goggles—those late-night accouterments that transform friends and strangers into hookup partners. I'd never heard about speed goggles, but as soon as Nate said it, I knew I wore them too.

How many times have I met a guy who offered nothing in terms of mate potential only to hear his PRs and think, *My, you're rather attractive*. I find out that someone who seemed stupid, old, and short can still run a 2:30 marathon? *Come on over, big boy*. You broke four minutes when you were in college? *You're cute*. Some will say you're only as good as your last race. I don't agree. I'll never run a 2:30 marathon or a 3:59 mile. I am attracted to people who can or did.

Being fast is about more than being fast; it's about commitment to an activity I value. I've heard that Frank Conroy, the late director of the prestigious Iowa Writer's Workshop, used to tell incoming students that writers needed two things: talent and character. The latter, he said, was harder to come by. There are plenty of runners with innate ability. But to be fast—to be excellent—requires something more. Something increasingly rare: it requires commitment.

I'm enough of a feminist not to need a man to take care of me, but enough of a girl to swoon at displays of power and accomplishment. Perhaps that's just human: we worship sports stars whose personal behavior and other attributes are often less than civilized. When I meet someone who does what I do, but better—much better—I tend to be impressed and will often, perhaps unfortunately, overlook less savory qualities. Sometimes talent is enough.

I'm always interested in how people talk about their PRS. When I worked in college admissions at Duke, I read an application from a kid who'd run a 4:18 mile. Ren's essay was about how he acquired his nickname, 2:10 Ren. A soccer player who got roped into running, Ren ran 2:10 in the 800 as a freshman. When I got to know him, he told me that he chose to write about his debut 800 rather than his mile time because, well, he was embarrassed. The combination of speed and modesty is winning. Frank Shorter apparently said that everyone ran 4:30 in high school. That tells you something about Frank Shorter, not about "everyone." (Frank Shorter is, however, pretty hot.)

I know lots of great and handsome men who slog through marathons at a slow and steady pace. It's not that I wouldn't go out with them, but when I see the cadaverous guys striding out before the gun goes off, my heart begins to race. It's possible that Khalid Khannouchi, Don Kardong, and Ian Torrence are not attractive men. I wouldn't know. They look darned good to me. Last summer I met a guy I wouldn't have talked to in a bar. Then I found out he was trying to break 2:30 at the St. George Marathon. What first seemed like skeletal geekiness was transformed into, well, you know. Speed goggles.

I've been divorced a long time and have gone on a lot of dates. I've given up on trying to find a STYF man; he's proved as elusive as an ivory-billed woodpecker. Plus, I've come to accept that I'm not everyone's cup of decaf skim chai: I don't cook, and I'm kind of mean. At this point, I'd settle for an interesting running partner who pushes me to keep up and never calls me "opinionated"; someone who teaches me new things and knows the value of a semicolon. If that's still too much to ask, maybe what I really need is a dog.

The Fast Young Man

12

He didn't run the race the day we met. He was there volunteering, figuring it was his turn to give back. I was volunteering too. It was a small club race, without official timing, and no awards. I'd seen his name before; he won lots of races. I'd never seen him, though. "That's you?" I said, when he told me who he was.

We talked for a while, mostly about books. We talked some about running, but mostly not. Mostly we talked about everything, the way you do when you meet someone whose soul you want to caress. It was seeing the aurora borealis when you are not expecting it, coming on a deer during a twilight run where you stop to gaze at each other. *Coup de foudre*. Lightning was desire.

We separated reluctantly that day—long after the runners had gone home, after the finish line had come down—he back to his wife, me to my boyfriend. I thought about him that night, about the lines around his eyes, the nervous set of his teeth, that he didn't know what to do with his hands.

His father, he had said, was a defrocked minister.

"What happened?"

"What usually happens to men of the cloth when they get into trouble? Nothing unusual or interesting."

He had married young. His wife had followed him to graduate school, earning their living by working at the university. She didn't run. He worked hard, trained hard. He was always tired, he said.

We saw each other a week later, at another race. That day he ran. He won. He scored a gift certificate to an upscale jewelry store, and we talked about it. I asked what he would spend it on. He guessed he'd get a gift for his wife. He asked me—or did I offer?—to come along and help him pick it out. I would, I said, if in exchange he would pace me through a fast mile on the track. Deal. We struck a deal.

We met at the jewelry store.

"Silver or gold?" I asked him.

"What?"

"Does she wear silver or gold?"

"I have no idea," he said.

"What's she like?"

"She's, well, I don't know."

"Plain or fancy? Funky or classic? What's her style?"

"I don't know," he said. "I've never thought about it."

They'd been married for four years. He didn't know if her ears were pierced. He seemed to think they were. I picked out a pair of simple silver earrings; she could trade them in if she didn't like them.

Was it a ruse? Now, knowing how nothing escaped his notice, how he remembered everything I ever said to him, the places we went, the qualities of light in the spaces we shared, the way the cinnamon-colored clay felt under our feet, the words I'd invent when nothing else sufficed—did he really not know, or was he telling me what I later knew he was telling me?

He started running at age seven. Living with his preacher father, mother, and two brothers out in the rural Carolina countryside, he watched as a bachelor farmer who lived down their road began running. A small seven-year-old—I can see him, all enthusiasm and curiosity and gentle questioning, all sharp elbows and long skinny legs—he would watch the guy go, at the same time each day, in overalls and tennis shoes.

"I thought he was doing something secret and special," he said. "I wanted to know what it was."

He began to trot along, a puppy on the heels of the big man who let him follow. Special and secret. His running has been like this.

From him I learned what it meant to take running seriously. To invest in being fast. I learned that his dissertation advisor, also a runner, didn't know that he ran. If the advisor knew how fast he was, he wouldn't take him seriously as an academic. He took it as axiomatic that everyone made the correlation between speed and an investment of time in training. It was news to me.

He ran twice a day. He worked late into the night. Sometimes he fell asleep while walking across campus. He was the first fast person I'd ever gotten to know and his routines fascinated me. I wanted to know what, exactly, he did on his runs. How far? How fast did he go? What did he eat? How did it feel to push himself? How did it feel to run that fast? Did it hurt? What did he do when it hurt?

I turned my training over to him, put myself in his hands. Sometimes, when he would tell me to run at a certain pace, he'd mean to say that I should run 7:15 miles, but instead he'd say 5:15, switching, inadvertently, his times for mine, him for me. He would give me things to think about: running forward, not back on the heels; moving quietly; pushing forward with the hips. When I asked him what got him through, he told me that he would tell himself that he was shit, that he sucked. He deserved to hurt. His self-talk was always negative. He'd gotten a tattoo years ago, years before all athletes had multicolor ink stains on their skin. He got it, he said, because he liked how it felt. He liked that it hurt.

I loved going to races with him, especially ones that had out-and-back courses where I could see him leading the pack home. I would not think about my own running, concentrating instead on how he was doing. At a certain point—fifteen minutes into a 5K race, half an hour into a 10K—I'd look at my watch and realize that he was done. Often he'd come back out on the course, especially at longer races, and run in with me. I always wanted to ask if he'd won, but I knew better.

He always won. I'd learned, intuited, not to ask that dreaded, loaded question. I'd ask how he did, what his time was. Finally, if he was being recalcitrant, I would get down to it and blurt out the words. Sometimes, if he was feeling cocky, he would answer: "Of course."

He had been invited to a new race in the Blue Ridge Mountains. I'd never been to the western part of the state I'd lived in for seven years. He'd been given a hotel room. He asked if I wanted to go. Lots of times he'd shared his freebie hotel rooms with other runners. It's just what you do, he said. He told his wife; I told my boyfriend. No big deal.

On the drive there I pressed him. I wanted to hear the way he thought about running, what it meant to him, how he worked his way through a race. I wanted to know what his training was like, what he ate, how much he slept. I needed him to be firmly in place as my running friend. That was explainable, uncontestable. I prized him as a runner. Were he not so fast, would I have found him so compelling?

He indulged me for a while, and then stopped. There would be no more talk of running. He switched gears and began telling stories, stories of his youth, of the region. He drawled out tales that should have come from a much older man, not from a graduate student. Each narrative showed another sparkling cut of his mind. A remarkable young man.

Young man, that's how I thought of him. He was twenty-seven to my thirty-six. But as with many runners, all those miles in the sun and the pounding of the body had aged him, made him craggy.

We settled into the hotel and then left again, embarrassed. We went out for dinner and had what he called a lucky drink.

One drink, and I was feeling loose. Back to the hotel room. Our room. Two beds. Home, at least for now. He let me use the bathroom first, and I tried to scrub the flush off my face; I undressed into shorts and a tee-shirt. He had waited to change until I came out, and then did his own ablutions. I could hear the water running, could hear him peeing. I got into my bed, farthest from the bathroom, and lay there, still and uncomfortable.

We talked for a while in the dark, offering revelations that come more freely under cover of warm night. We listened to each other breathe. If we had been in the same bed, touching, his hard body against mine, that would have been different. Maybe. Being with him in the dark, in that clean and simple hotel room, felt like something secret, something special.

The next morning he dressed early and waited for me in the lobby.

We were planning to warm up together, but I told him to go on. It was too much.

The race was scenic, as promised. As I was finishing, there he was, cheering me in loudly, more loudly than I would have thought possible for him, so soft spoken, so gentle. I heard his voice, and it drew me to the finish. He jogged up, gave me a bottle of water, and draped his arm lightly over my shoulders.

I wanted to know about his race—what was his time, where did he finish? I knew the field was tough. He was the first American, in a blistering time, at a pace faster than I could ever hope to run even one mile. Faster, even, than I could run a half mile.

After the awards ceremony—he gave me his prize, a Lucite block—we went back to the hotel to take our separate showers and change into clean clothes. Then we set off to hike up the ridges of the mountains. We ambled along and then sat for a couple of hours on a rock, in the sun, side by side and talked fuzzy, tired talk. At times, when making a point, he would touch my arm, my leg.

"We should go," I said, as the sun began to sink. He looked at me.

"We should go," I said.

He touched my cheek.

"We should go."

"Yes," he said, finally. "We should."

That night, I went out to a nice restaurant with my boyfriend, an older man, an established academic. He came in with his wife. They were, improbably, seated at the table closest to us. He sat right next to me. I faced his wife. There were uncomfortable moments, and then my oblivious, obliging boyfriend extended a hand, introduced himself and said, "Haven't you two been spending enough time together?" I noticed that his wife was wearing the earrings I'd picked out.

We continued to hook up for runs, meeting at the trailhead. My heart thudded when I saw his car; my stomach clenched when I saw him. His cheeks were hollow, and he chattered his teeth, rodent-like. Not a beautiful man. But I'd watch him changing out of his grownup work clothes discretely between two open car doors. We bantered, had easy exchanges: *How was your day? Things okay on the home front?* Once I'd shown up after work wearing mascara and lipstick and he laughed at me. "You don't wear makeup when you're running," he said. "Serious runners don't wear makeup."

He'd jog with me after already putting in a hard 10 miles. I'd still have to struggle to keep up. I wanted to hear his track workout times, to know his splits. My own seemed paltry, my ambitions frail.

He'd run a fast marathon before, under two and a half hours, but not fast enough for him to tell me his exact time. He had injuries he didn't like to talk about. It wasn't clear when he'd be able to attempt his next marathon. But I knew that I wanted to do another. And I wanted to go farther—to do an ultramarathon. He laughed about the big-legged trail runners who ran these ridiculously long distances.

It was his birthday, his twenty-eighth. He said that since college he'd run his years in miles, celebrating aging the way he lived, by running. But there was no reason, he said, to go farther than 26.2.

And so for his birthday, he decided he needed to find a cinder track, not the new rubberized kind, but the old-fashioned type that he had run on in high school, and speed through twenty-eight quarters. He asked me to help him find the track. I asked around and discovered one at a defunct elementary school in a run-down neighborhood. We went there, after work, and I timed him. I had to sprint across the field in order to give him the splits at 200 meters. He ran twenty-eight quarter miles in sixty-two seconds each.

It didn't seem to tax him, though when he was done he said, as he did after each race, "That was hard."

After, we sat in the middle of the field. I picked blades of grass, twirled them around my fingers, and tied them into knots. I made a long chain and wrapped it around his wrist, so thin, so bony.

"Happy birthday," I said.

He was going out for dinner that night with his wife.

We traveled to races throughout the summer. I was getting faster and stronger, and our time together was getting harder. I had broken up with my boyfriend. He was still with his wife. We were running buddies. I was in love with him. He was, I'm fairly certain, in love with me. This was not, I knew, a way to live. I continued to train hard; trained so that it hurt.

After my spring disaster at Camp Lejeune, I wanted to redeem myself. I was going to be in California in the fall for work and noticed that the Silicon Valley Marathon, in its beta version, would be taking place at around the time I was scheduled to be in San Jose.

He wrote me a marathon program. It was less rigid than Peter's, and more attuned to how I lived my life—he knew I could only do what was possible, even if it was not ideal. I followed his plan exactly. I went to the track for half-mile repeats; did my long runs at the pace he suggested, sometimes with him, sometimes on my own, sometimes with the group in Duke Forest.

I went to California for my work trip, ready for a marathon. I called him on the phone the night before the race. Even with the difference in time, he was at his office. He was always at his office.

"You will feel so good for so long," he said.

"It won't even be hard until mile 20," he said.

"You can do it," he said.

And I did. The first half clipped by—the miles clicking off so fast I could hardly believe it. I heard his voice—"You will feel so good for so long"—and I did. *Swing the arms, drive the elbows back. Relax the face, the jaw, the neck. Drop the shoulders. Turnover is quick, the legs are moving gracefully, easily. No trouble breathing—check for tightness. Left Achilles, maybe a little sore? No, breathe into it. This is what you do. This is what you are. Run.*

When I finished in 3:24, I said to myself, "That was hard."

I called Andrew and Mike and they asked me to read them the splits off my watch. They cheered for every mile faster than 7:30, and for those that were over 8:00 they made excuses: "Must have been a hill." "You were probably getting water."

Then I called him.

He said, "I knew you could do it."

Once when I'd asked him what he thought about when it got really hard in a race, what idea he could rely on to get him through, he looked at me from under a furrowed brow and said, quietly, "I can take more pain than anyone else."

We stopped running together. I stopped it.

I e-mailed him, when it seemed time, to tell him that I still thought about him.

How can that be? He wanted to know. You've never written about me, he said.

I still think about him. Still carry him with me, years later now, at every race.

Boston

13

If the South is about the nineteenth century—the crucible of the Civil War never far from the public imagination and referred to by some, still, as the war of Northern aggression—New England, and in particular Boston, is about the eighteenth, with sinners still in the hands of an angry God erecting statues to the heroes of the Revolutionary War.

It is a place that celebrates the midnight ride of Paul Revere, the battles of Lexington and Concord, the party in the harbor, and, on the third Monday in April, Patriot's Day, when everyone in the state of Massachusetts is off from work and school. It's a day the Red Sox always play at home, and when, for the last hundred and something years, the Boston Marathon is run.

Who runs the Boston Marathon?

Those who qualify.

Who qualifies?

The fast. And the old. The older you are, the less fast you need to be. A seventy-year-old man can qualify with 4:30; a seventy-year-old woman with five hours.

Also the philanthropic. Those who raise money for charity can run.

And the doctors. Doctors can run, even if they are slow, if they are members of the American Medical Athletic Association, pony up over a thousand bucks, and go to a CME—Continuing Medical Education—seminar.

And the bandits. Boston has a long history of allowing unregistered runners to start at the end of the pack and run. This, of course, does not count.

Mostly, it's the fast.

How fast? Men under thirty-five need to be able to run 3:10. Actually, it's 3:10:59. They give you the seconds up to the next tick of the clock. For women under thirty-five, it's 3:40. The time escalates five minutes with each five-year age group up to fifty. Then you get fifteen minutes for aging up (though men get only ten between fifty-four and fifty-five).

How fast is 3:10? That's 7:15 miles. The youngest women have to clock in with 8:24s.

Qualifying times are good for eighteen months. Nothing says you have to be in the same shape to run Boston as you were to enter it. Lots of people go with cameras and the expectation of enjoying a comfortable jog through history; taking it easy, having a good time, if not a fast time.

But getting to the line is difficult, not only because you have to qualify, but because you have to get there. The race starts in the little town of Hopkinton, 26.2 miles away from the center of the Hub. That means waking early to board buses—yellow, hard-seated school buses from districts all around the city. Like all things relating to the Boston Marathon, it's a meritocracy, not a democracy. You board according to your number, which reflects your qualifying time. The fastest people get the goodies. Then everyone spends a number of hours hanging out, waiting for the start.

Special people get a dot.

The dot gets stuck on your number and it means VIP. It's good to be a VIP.

You get to wait in a heated tent for the upholstered buses to take you, later, to Hopkinton. Instead of milling around in the mud and the muck of the school yard with the hoi polloi, the dotted ones get to wait inside the school, with hot coffee and tea, bagels, and dedicated porta-potties.

You can look out onto the masses, huddled on blankets, shivering in the cold or being baked by the sun, and lined up for miles to pee. And thank the Lord, or the Hancock (a major sponsor), or your colleagues who know the big shots, for your dot. You can see, as the start time nears, the giant pile of discarded clothing growing. There are thousands of empty water bottles. There are lots of people eager to run into Boston.

The dot makes things more comfortable. But really, it is the Athlete's Village, the scene outside the school in Hopkinton, that makes Boston special: the conversations about where you qualified, the comparisons of other marathons, the friendships formed in the porta-potty lines. Having a dot is nice, but not having one is fine too.

Recently the hallowed start time of high noon has been moved up, and now the race starts in waves—the wheelchair athletes first, and then elite women. They've cut off two hours of Hopkinton hang-out time. It's a shame, really, because that was part of the experience of the race. Getting sunburned and dehydrated before you even start to run; freezing and risking hypothermia before the gun goes off. Now it's more like a regular marathon.

Except, of course, that it's nothing like a regular marathon. It's Boston. It's the Nobel Prize of marathoning, the Harvard of running, the QE2 of races. It's the Coliseum, the Louvre Museum, the melody of a symphony by Strauss. It's a lyric by Cole Porter.

Part of what makes it special is primogeniture, the riches that come to the first-born. That it's the oldest is helpful. But there are plenty of long-standing institutions we've done away with for the good of all. Slavery, for example. And there are plenty of old things that have lost their luster. Think olive green refrigerators and girdles. But Boston's history works for it.

The course works. It shows off the region to good effect. You start with a screaming downhill, a fast start for fast runners, on a small country road in the about-to-bloom spring of New England. There aren't many spectators until you get to mile 2, where leather-backed gorillas sit on their Harleys, Buds in hands, and cheer. You run from one town to the next, with their quaint and welcoming signs: *Entering Framingham* (crossing the train tracks), *Entering Natick* (passing Lake Cochituate), *Entering Wellesley*. You hear Wellesley before you get to it. The women of the college create a "screech tunnel," and screech they do. It's girls gone wild, cheering loudly for all, but loudest for their distaff comrades. You're halfway home, but the hardest part is ahead.

The heartbreak starts at the Newton Fire Station, when you turn onto Commonwealth Avenue. A series of four hills from miles 17 to 21 culminates in the famously titled one. You will have been warned: It's not that the hills are that bad, but they come at a bad time in the race. You run alongside the T, the "trolley" that is Boston's public transportation. It is perhaps better not to know that a marathon bib on the third Monday in April will suffice for fare. You hear but do not listen to the siren call. Odysseus had himself lashed to the mask. You must lash yourself, keep eyes ahead.

At this point, in the tony neighborhoods, people clot the streets. They come out every year, these spectators, often stationing themselves at the same place, tailgating, drinking, encouraging. They know enough not to tell you that "you're almost there" when you're not. They are astute marathon-watchers, the best in the world. They'll say your stride looks even, that your pace is strong. They'll warn that there's one more hill and then you can rest for a while. They'll tell you that you're doing a good job. At this point, it feels like work.

The Citgo sign beckons. It's not a gas station, but a beacon. You can see it for miles, it seems, and feel like you'll never reach it. You run through the urban names: Cleveland Circle, Chestnut Hill, Kenmore

Square, and finally you get to the Citgo sign itself. If, at mile 21 you feel good, you cruise in on a slight downhill. If you feel good at 21, you're golden. But if you abused yourself on those early downhill miles, got caught up in the frenzy, the suffering will be compounded by the public nature of your fall. Compassionate shouts from spectators will make you want to hang your head in shame. *Don't look at me,* you'll want to scream back at them. And they'll keep telling you, "Good job." And, in truth, "You're almost there."

The unicorn, on its blue and yellow ribbon, will hang weighty on your neck. No matter how many marathon medallions you have collected in other places, this one will feel substantial.

That night, the next day, hobbling around the city, making your way through the airport, walking the stiff-legged walk of the marathoner, locals will not ask you if you ran the race. They will ask your time. What did you think of the course? Did you go out too fast at the start? Will you be coming back next year?

The locals are what make this race special. And the runners. And the course. And the history. And the volunteers. And, for us lucky few with well-connected friends, the dot.

14

Becoming a Marathoner

Andrew rented a sports utility vehicle because, he said, this was a sporting event. We—me and my two ex-boyfriends—were driving around Boston. Andrew is a bad driver in the best of circumstances, and anyone who has ever driven in Boston knows that Beantown traffic conditions are trying at best. I tried tactfully to direct him—"Watch out for the &*^#$ pedestrians!" "You're driving off the @#$*&^ road!" "You're the world's worst driver!" Mike attempted to keep us calm. I was going to run my first Boston. Calm was a long way off.

We stayed with my friends Michael and Lorna. Michael was the best friend of my college boyfriend Chuck. I'd dumped Chuck but retained a share in Michael. I knew that he and Andrew and Mike would get each other's jokes, find each other's stories interesting, and they did. Andrew showed Mike his old collegiate haunting grounds, and they visited the Boston Museum of Science, outside of which stands a large audio-kinetic sculpture made by my stepfather, George Rhoads. They ate at Legal Sea Foods, walked along the Charles, had a great time. I stayed in and read novels while swigging water and eating pretzels. Peter had forecast dire consequences if I trotted around town the day before a race.

Before I went to sleep, I laid out my clothes, pinned my number onto my shirt, and thought that 26 miles is a long way to run. I did not sleep well.

Nor did I run well. I felt good for the first half—the downhill miles—and then I felt very bad. I made the classic, tragic mistake of going out too fast, and I paid, in classic, tragic fashion, for my hubris. I was shamed.

Mike and Andrew knew by the clock that I was likely to be in a bad mood at the finish. I did not disappoint them. The sole person I disappointed was me, the only one who cared about my time.

I trained hard the next year. I was determined, dedicated, and diligent. I decided that I would go back alone; I didn't want witnesses to my dissolution.

Because I'd started writing for *Running Times*, I worked the booth at the expo, answering questions and trying to stay off my feet. I spent two hours standing over Bill Rodgers's shoulder while he signed autographs. The line snaked for miles, and I was charged with trying to keep it moving. Fat chance.

A guy would come up to Bill, poster in hand, ready for signing, and say: "I ran in the same 10K as you in Tiny Town, Illinois, in 1983." Bill would get that dopey look he sometimes wears. He'd blink, think for a minute, and say: "Yeah, Tiny Town. It was really hot that day" (the guy would nod enthusiastically) "and I was racing against Frank" (nodding frantically now) "and then there was a last turn into town and that's where I took him." Then Boston Billy would look the guy dead in the eye, and you'd have thought the race was yesterday—or that he and the man from Tiny Town had been best friends for the intervening years.

I watched as Bill did this again and again, with every person, remembering folks he'd met this way years earlier. I sat at the feet of the master, and, though I'd never before asked anyone for an autograph, at the end of the day I asked him to sign my race number. It says: "Rachel. Run fast. Write lots. Bill Rodgers."

I was staying in Boston with the parents of a student whose application to Duke I'd read when I worked as an admissions officer and who I had gotten to know when he arrived on campus. The mom—Mia Farrowesque, slender and gracious—greeted me after the race at the door of their large apartment on Commonwealth Avenue, just around the corner from the finish. "Oh Rachel," she said, "you're done much earlier than I expected." I loved her at that moment. I'd finished in 3:18, faster than her husband or son had ever run it.

She drew me a bath the size of a small bedroom, filled it with potions from Canyon Ranch, brought me drinks and fruit, and told me how impressed she was with me. On the course, I'd seen a group of boys from the Roxbury Latin School. They had all just been accepted to Duke, and I was the agent of their admission. They held up a sign that said: "RL loves Duke." And then, my name and my number. I had seen the big sign, heard their cheering voices just as I started climbing the Newton Hills, and I swear, by God I swear, it made me faster.

I crawled out of the lap of luxury and walked back over to the finish. I watched people coming in as five hours showed on the clock. While for some it did look hard, others were clearly elated and having a wonderful time. Unlike the last few silent miles I'd run with my cohort, these folks were still yukking it up, still stopping to take photos, still happy. I saw that life at the back of the pack is different. Not better, not worse. Different.

That fall I ran my fastest time, 3:14, in Raleigh, North Carolina. It was a hometown race, and I had my hometown friends there with me. It was only after that, after my fifth, that I would call myself a marathoner.

Now they tend to run together. I've done more than forty marathons and ultras and have won a handful of small boutiquey races in mountainous, out-of-the-way places: the foothills of the Sierra Nevada; Mount Mitchell, North Carolina; Bozeman, Montana; and, on the third day of a 100-mile stage race, the Mount Everest Challenge Marathon in the Himalayas.

I had decided I was about done with road races and wanted to concentrate on trail runs and ultras when I was asked to lead a pace group for the inaugural More Marathon, the first-ever marathon only for women over forty. I couldn't say no, especially as I would be taking the 3:50 (read: Boston qualifying time) group. I wanted to say no—it was five laps of Central Park. But when I saw all these strong, fit women ready to run, I knew it would be a memorable experience. When we passed (five times) a guy holding a sign that said, "You don't look a day over twenty-nine." I said, "No. This is what forty—or forty-two, or fifty-two, or eighty-one—looks like." Strong, fit, and, yes, beautiful. We ran past Roger Robinson, a world-class runner and writer. After hearing him shout out kind words about an article I'd just done for *Running Times*, I felt like I could lead my women to Albany, to Canada even.

Then I heard Roger's wife call my name, and I filled with emotion. Kathrine Switzer is an iconic figure for us women marathoners: The image of Jock Semple trying to pull her off the course after she'd shed her hooded sweatshirt to become the first woman to officially run Boston is indelible for those of us who do not take the gains of feminism for granted. Kathrine paved the way, with beauty and grace, strength and guts, to become the perfect ambassador for the sport. I pointed her out to my women, but they didn't need me to—they knew exactly who she was. We were all fueled by Kathrine's presence.

Then we got giddy. At mile 23 we started singing show tunes. One of the women could sing "Doe a Deer" in Spanish. My group crossed the line in 3:48:59. I'd run the whole marathon holding a wooden dowel with balloons on it announcing, in Sharpie marker, my finish time. It was a windy day and the balloons kept bonking me on the head. Toward the end of the race, I used them to shoo runners coming in the opposite direction out of the way. Afterward, I didn't want to put down my balloons. I wanted to hold on to that unforgettable experience.

Having lived in the City for eight years without ever running a step, once I became a marathoner, I had, of course, to run the New York Marathon. It was everything I knew it would be. I'd scored a sub-elite number and got to start on the upper level of the Verrazano Narrows Bridge, toe to toe with the elite men (the elite woman had started earlier). It was exciting to be up at the front, if momentarily, and it was fun to run only with women for the first 8 miles. As much as Boston is about history, New York is about culture; running though all five boroughs, we were able to see how quickly, how dramatically, the neighborhoods changed. It was an astonishing tour of the city.

Indeed, if I had to pick one marathon, the most unforgettable, the first among equals, it would be New York. But not the first year I actually ran it. The year before.

I was training for a December marathon and happened to be in the City the weekend of New York. I decided that I'd do a 20-mile run at marathon pace, jumping into the race in Park Slope, Brooklyn, my former stomping grounds. I do not approve of bandits. Running without a number may be a time-honored tradition in Boston, but then so is driving like a maniac. That doesn't make it acceptable in other places. I decided I would take no aid along the course and would bail out long before the finish line. And I had a secret plan to make myself feel less like a thief.

My friend Sarah and I walked down from her apartment to Fourth Avenue. I'd done the math to know what time I had to be there in order to join those who were running my pace. Just as I was saying goodbye to Sarah and was about to duck under the barricade and step into the race, I heard my name. It was my ex-husband's best friend from childhood. I'd not seen him for years. By the time we caught up, it was too late for me to join the folks who were clicking off 7:30s. I started to run, trying to be as unobtrusive as possible, but it was a game of weaving and wending through the crowd.

It was hard to concentrate on running. I've always had a guilty conscience (unfounded, I swear) and often my heartbeat quickens when I see a police officer, assuming that I'm about to get busted for something. It was different now, in November 2001, in New York City.

The cops were heroes. They were there to serve, even if they were not able to protect. Who could protect us from the unimaginable?

The City was raw. It has always had a gritty, definitional urbanness; New York is the ne plus ultra of cities. But it was different now. You could still smell the smoke: rancid, charry air mixed with the fall colors. When you looked downtown, you saw what was not there; you could no longer orient yourself to the south by the buildings that used to tower over all others.

I needed to be there. I had flown up from my home in Durham to stay with Val—hugging her, touching her, rejoicing that a few years before she had left her job in the World Trade Center and now worked in midtown. She'd called me from her office that morning, narrating what she could see of horrors only a few miles away. I passed through Grand Central Station on my way to her apartment. There was a large bulletin board where the missing notices were posted. They were like an accident. You couldn't stand to look at them, and you couldn't stand not to look. Some were hastily handwritten in broken English, others were finessed by scanned photographs and carefully articulated descriptions of a husband, wife, partner, son, or daughter.

Conversations with friends and strangers started the same way: Where were you when? I was 500 miles away, glued, like the rest of the nation, to TV coverage that felt uncomfortably like a disaster movie that wouldn't end. Manhattan seemed both far away and around the corner. Being back, talking with friends, catastrophe was tangible—you could smell it. *Where were you when?* The need to tell the stories was as strong as the desire to bear witness. *Where were you when?*

There was something else that was different, as different as seeing American flags draped everywhere, of cynical lefties flying patriotic colors, as different as understanding that our world would never be the same. People had changed. The vaunted New York chilliness—the city where almost forty years before people heard Kitty Genovese being killed but did nothing to stop it, the place where suited-and-tied businessmen stepped unseeingly over homeless people, where you could live in an apartment building for decades and not know one of your neighbors—had warmed. Community was built out of the ashes of the magnificently tall buildings that had fallen. When I remarked to a friend that there were lots of American flags flying in North Carolina but not nearly as many as on his street in Brooklyn he said, flatly, "It was our town they attacked." New York City had become a town.

I ran my way through the crowds, trying to be unobtrusive. At mile 20 I saw her. I'd decided it would be a woman. That was part of the plan. I heard her say to a guy she'd been running with—"I'm fine, go ahead." She was smiling, and running strong.

I sidled up to her.

"You know what they say about 'the wall' at mile 20?"

"Yes?" She looked apprehensive.

"It's a myth. No such thing. Don't worry about it."

She smiled. She laughed.

"I'm Rachel," I said.

Her name was Liz. It was written on the front of her shirt. This was her first marathon. She was the mother of three, lived in the suburbs, and had been training for the race by herself. "It's something I wanted to do just for me," she said. "It's a special time in my day, the time I get to run."

Her husband and children had VIP seats at the finish and would be waiting for her there, she said. She was feeling pretty good, she said, though getting a little tired. I asked what her husband did, and when she told me that he was a financial guy who worked in the City, I waited. She told me the story—the hours of waiting to hear, the relief in getting a phone call. We talked about that day in September, the same conversations, but somehow different. Running this race was a way of celebrating.

The cheers of Wellesley students paled in comparison to the screams of marathoners when they passed by fire brigades. For once, the race wasn't about the runners but about those whose strength, courage, and endurance made our efforts look trivial. We cheered for them as we passed, and they cheered right back. The firefighters, human memorials, gave us support and energy.

But not enough to counteract the sobering effect of knowing who we were running with. Too many people wore signs that read "In memory of ——." In honor of ——. They told their stories on their backs—"I trained to run this race with my dad. I love you, Dad. I miss you. 9.11." Photographs. Names. Tears.

We ran to celebrate. We ran to get away from the knowledge we carried with us, saturating us as cloyingly as the smoke that clung to our clothes. We talked, Liz and I. She told me about her family, her kids. As the miles ticked by and Liz began to tire, I talked. I told her stories. I confessed to this soccer mom that without my ex-boyfriends I would subsist entirely on popcorn, neither able nor willing to cook for myself.

I regaled her with stories of Emma, the Vietnamese pot-bellied pig Andrew and I had gotten years after we'd broken up, told how we co-parented the little force of nature and how her behavior changed depending on whose house she was at (with me, she was the very picture of porcine deportment; at Andrew's she was a spoiled-rotten little swine). I talked to her about the job I'd quit, shared tales from the frontlines of the college admissions battle. Her kids were young enough for her not to be overly worried, but old enough for her to want to know the scoop. I told her I that I'd written a book on college admissions and that I lived in Durham.

I encouraged her as we ran, gave little pointers (*try not to clench your fists, drink more water*), but generally I did what I do best: babble. I drenched Liz with an effortless, endless stream of words, some better and more funny than others, in an attempt to keep her mind off her body.

We crossed from the Bronx into Spanish Harlem, cheered by legions of spectators in a variety of languages. We ran down Fifth Avenue comfortably. Just before the course took a right turn into Central Park,

I told Liz that she was doing great and that I was going to keep heading south on Fifth. I didn't want to go near the finish line.

"DON'T LEAVE ME."

She screamed it out and grabbed a fistful of the back of my shirt.

"Okay, okay," I said, surprised by her vehemence and trying to figure out where the course went. We were in the park now—but would soon, I realized, spill back out onto the street, to run on Central Park South. I could get out at Columbus Circle leaving Liz with less than half a mile to the finish.

We ran past a clock.

When we first started running together, I asked Liz what her goal was.

"To finish," is what she said. Of course that's what she said. She's a woman.

"Really," I said, "how fast do you want to run this thing?"

She demurred, but I pushed her and she conceded that her dream was to break four hours.

At that point, I had no idea what kind of pace we were on. When I saw the clock at mile 24, I knew that she could do it.

"Listen to me," I said to Liz. "Focus your eyes on my back and just follow. Stay with me. Don't think about anything except following me."

She was getting to the point in the marathon where you lose the ability to speak in complete sentences but she grunted assent.

I picked up the pace and began to slink through openings created by the space between other runners. It was still crowded and we had to make our way through struggling, slowing bodies. I paved the way and Liz followed.

I'd cast a glance over my shoulder to make sure she was still there. She was. "You okay?"

"Yes."

"Good. Stay with me."

"Okay."

One thing about women: they often take direction well.

We came out onto Central Park South, the last straightaway before the turn back into the park.

"Liz, listen. You can make it under four. You've run your first marathon, and you're going to do it in under four hours. Don't slow down. I have to leave you here, but you've got it. It's in the bag. Just go."

"Thank you, thank you," she said, and she went.

I scooted under the barricade and headed downtown. I had another 2 miles to get back to Val's apartment, but I'd accomplished my mission. I told myself that if I was going to use the race for my own training purposes without actually entering it, I'd find a way to give back. Liz's desperate cry when I told her I was going to leave convinced me that I had done my part, a small part, a small gesture. Heading downtown in New York City in the fall of 2001, small gestures seemed important. Caring for each other, seeing commonalities instead of differences— these were the lessons of those months after September 11.

Returning to Durham was like walking out into a sunny day after seeing a depressing matinee. No more smell of smoke, no more "missing" posters, no more first-person stories to hear of horrors and secondhand accounts of lives disrupted beyond belief.

I returned to a flashing answering machine. One of the callers said her name was Liz. She said she'd run the New York Marathon that Sunday and that when she crossed the line—in under four hours—she told her husband that at the end of the race she was so exhausted she'd been hallucinating. She'd read that this sometimes happened. Liz told her husband that she had imagined that an angel had come down from heaven to run the last 6 miles with her.

"That was no angel," her husband said, laughing. "I have a photograph of the two of you running together."

I had told her only my first name. She tracked me down because she wanted to thank me, to thank me for helping her make her dream come true.

I listened to that message five times.

I thought not of the smell of smoke, the impromptu shrines that had appeared all over the city, the Portraits of Grief section of the *New York Times* that daily told the stories of the lost. Instead I thought of how the course of the New York Marathon goes through five boroughs, and in running it you see the flavor of neighborhoods change by the block: Irish and Italians waving their flags; Hassidic Jews, prayer shawl fringe flapping as they clapped their hands; Spanish-speakers from legions of different countries; African Americans who've lived for generations in this city; newly arrived immigrants from all over the world; Arabs, Asians, blue-blooded Park Avenue ladies, college students.

They all came out that day to cheer us on. They cheered for Liz, and they cheered for me, as I cheered for her, by her side. Our voices blended in unity, at least for a handful of hours.

Racing

15

Don't look back.

The directive could not have been more simple or more clear. You can go to hell, Orpheus, and collect your beloved Eurydice. Bring her back from the dead. You can return to earth from the underworld. She will follow you. But don't look back.

He looked back. And he lost her.

It's hard to lead a race. The fact is, it's awful. The one thing they tell you is: Don't look back. It takes energy, messes with your stride, interferes with your forward motion. But it does something else as well. It betrays a lack of confidence, a lack of faith. It makes obvious the fact that you're running scared.

I never got the hang of racing. I don't have in me the desire to hurt. I think, often, of my fast young man who said, "I can take more pain than anyone." I can't, nor do I want to. But I do like to win. Sometimes I get lucky.

Rarely do I show up at the starting line and expect to race, let alone to win. Most of the time I think, *I'll just jog along, talk to strangers, enjoy the scenery.* And then the gun goes off. I'll look ahead, see how many women are in front of me, and make a mental note. Most of the races I do are long, and I tell myself to take it easy, to run at my own pace, not to worry about competing. Most of the time I don't listen to myself. I get twitchy. I start caring about how many women are in front of me. I pick up the pace. Then it's best to find someone to chat away the early miles with. There will be time later to race, if it comes to that.

In trail races, it's hard to know how far ahead or behind the next runners are. Once at a 50K in Oregon, I came to an aid station about halfway through the race and another woman was there, filling up her water bottles. She looked at me with such surprise and horror that I felt I should apologize. She gathered herself and sprinted away. In the years since, I have looked at other runners, other women, in the same way.

It's hard and scary to lead a race. Better to chase than to be chased, better to be predator than prey. The anxiety alone—*How far back is she? I'm starting to tire, is she? I can't keep this up much longer*—is enough to add minutes to your time, to add burden to your load. Some people thrive on this. It helps them to push themselves harder than they thought possible. It can result in faster times.

It's the idea behind "rabbits," runners who set a pace and, for some predetermined distance, lead the race. No one wants to lead. The rabbit, often paid, takes the duty so that the competitors can relax early on. Eventually, the rabbit drops out and then it becomes a real race. Someone has to lead it. Many groups of Kenyan runners, and indeed, members of teams who train together, will take turns being in front. It's considered good form. It's part of the social contract.

Sometimes I've had men pace me through a race. At my fastest marathon, my buddies Scott and Ralph ran with me and encouraged me, blocked the wind, and allowed me to train my eyes on their backs, stop thinking, and follow, just as I did for Liz, that November day in New York City. I've now done this for lots of people at lots of marathons. But getting paced to finish in a good time is different from racing. To have a man pace me like this all the way through a race I was hoping to win would be, well, cheating.

Men and women may be running in the same race, but we are not racing.

This is not always clear. Especially to men.

I wondered what could have possessed my friend—let's call him Butch—to say, at the beginning of a half marathon, that his goal was to be the first woman. Was this hyper-competitive man trying to get in touch with his feminine side? Was he divulging a secret of confused gender identity? Was he making a funny?

"You want to be the first woman?" I had to ask.

Butch looked at me like I was crazy. "What are you, crazy?" he said, bouncing up and down on his toes, waking up his wiry, long-muscled legs. "I never said that. I want to *beat* the first woman."

Ah. That made sense. Except, of course, that it didn't.

Once I heard him correctly, I realized that Butch was expressing a fairly common, if unsettling, sentiment. I immediately thought of watching the New York City Marathon on television in 1998, when eventual winner Franca Fiacconi ran too much of the race with some random guy clipping her heels. Maybe he wanted to be able to say that he had run with the leader of the women's race. Maybe he wanted to leech some moments of TV fame. Maybe he was just grateful to have someone to run with, because, as we know, New York can be a lonely place. Whatever his intention, you could see all the way from your own living room that the guy was driving Fiacconi nuts. Finally she turned to him, said things in Italian best left untranslated and made a gesture that was universally understood.

Men and women may well be running in the same race, but the truth is, we are not racing against each other. Indeed, in the most important events—world championships, Olympic Games—the races are not coed. Some of the big marathons are now allowing an earlier elite women's start, making it easier for the fleetest of distaff foot to race unencumbered by male hangers-on and distracters. It also helps to keep the women's race clear of charges of pacing from helpful men.

When I first started racing, I was a solid middle-of-the-packer. Toward the end of long races, men I passed would encourage me, calling out "Nice work," or "Looking good." I was grateful for their generosity of spirit.

When I got more serious and began running harder—and longer—things changed. While the women I passed were still gracious, the men waxed less supportive the closer I got to the front of the field. Perhaps it was because we were all running harder, because it hurts more at the end when you're pushing. Not many of us want to talk then. But perhaps something else was going on.

At the finish of more races than I can recall, I've been approached by men I never noticed who either thank me for pulling them along, or who confess that they'd tried their damnedest to beat me but couldn't. I wondered at first if there was something odd and memorable about me. Did they say this to other men? Sometimes, maybe. But the fact is, as a woman, I stood out—a moving target.

A few of my male friends used to keep closer tabs on my race results than I did. After races, I often heard, "Next time, I'm going to get you."

My response was always the same: "I'm not racing against you."

Even were I to win a race outright, I would still get the trophy for first woman, not first person. Women winning races is becoming increasingly common in the longer distances, especially in trail ultras. But in every race, there are at least two competitions going on; within those are the less-apparent battles for masters or age-group awards. (It's not so easy to tell the difference between a thirty-nine-year-old woman and a forty-year-old.) But that doesn't stop some guys from sprinting to beat me to the finish.

Saturday mornings I used to run with a bunch of faster guys who would knock themselves out in training, fueled by testosterone and trash-talk. They would kindly wait for me as I slogged along to keep up. I neither could nor wanted to compete on my weekend long runs. I saved my hard running for races.

At a 50K, I saw one of my training partners just ahead at an aid station. Oh goody, I thought, we can run together and have a chance to catch up (ultras are like that). But as soon as he saw me, he took off like a deer during hunting season. I kept up my pace and watched as he began running with another woman. They kept turning around and looking at me, trailing them by no more than 100 yards.

When I passed my buddy, he was hanging onto a tree, catching his breath. We said a quick hello, and I kept going. When I caught up to the woman he'd been running with, we chatted for a while and I told her my name.

"I know, I know," she said. "I've heard all about you." I asked if my friend had been giving her pointers on how to race against me. "Hell, no," she said. "All he could talk about was not letting you beat him. He said if you caught him on a downhill, it would be all over. He really didn't want you to beat him."

"Good job," she said, as I went by.

"You too," I said and pushed on toward the finish.

I wanted to be the first woman.

The Western State · 16

You know the Saul Steinberg cartoon of the view of the world from New York City? It's the one where Manhattan is huge and the rest of the world is barely squeezed into the background. Regionalism, friends, is strong in this country.

I was once one of those parochial New Yorkers. During my first years in Durham, North Carolina, I traded my black clothes, martinis, and cigarettes for running shorts, Gatorade, and Gu. As I shed the trappings of urban life, I tried to strip away the prejudices endemic to New Yorkers. I learned that the South is a complex place, its placid surfaces often belying a rich intensity. I also learned that the South has as much regional jingoism as anywhere. One of the most damning things you can say to an outsider is, "You're not from around here, are you?"

Regional pride runs deep, too, in California.

California. I spent my last summer as a thirty-something in the foothills of the northern Sierra Nevada. Milton wrote, "Space may produce new worlds." He wasn't kidding. The brown and shrubby hills created a new me, hewn tough in shrubby manzanita and gold dust. The California mountains, like many of the Californians I met, are sharp and strong. There's a freshness, an untrammeled quality that is a counterpoise to the jaded, worn-out cynicism of a lot of us East Coasters. The edges have not been smoothed out, on the people or the places.

Traces of the frontier spirit are still visible in the West. They are manifest in a gameness, a disregard of tradition. I asked Gordy Ainsleigh why he decided to run the Western States trail nearly thirty years ago. His horse had come up lame for the Tevis Cup, and by running the 100-mile course in the same sub-twenty-four-hour time as the top horses, he essentially created the sport of ultramarathon trail running.

"Because they said it couldn't be done," he said, as if it were a stupid question. This is a California man, born and bred.

In Gordy's wake sprung a host of trail races in the West. His neighborhood, the area around Auburn, California, where the Western States 100-miler ends, is perhaps the epicenter of trail running. It's home not only to some of the biggest and best ultras—the American River 50 miler, the Way Too Cool 50K, and innumerable other, smaller ones—but also to some of the most awe-inspiring runners of the trail.

There's a great and good sense of community among the people who spend weekends together, competing against each other but really, against the terrain that they love so much. There's a pride of place that emanates from their belief that they live in paradise. In a region that hosts a shocking number of 100-mile races, no one is impressed when you say that you are going out to do a 25-mile training run.

People's work lives seem less essential than they do back East. There are few hints of educational snobbery. People read, or they don't. They watch TV, or they don't. They eat their avocados and think you're nuts if you claim, rightly, that these are slimy and repulsive things.

The Californians are out on the trails, in rain, snow, sleet, and hail. The heat of the day does not keep them at home. Men in races are accustomed to being routinely trounced by their female companions. Western women pee standing up.

I had been asked to house- and horse-sit for friends who lived in a tiny miner's cabin in the suburbs of Nevada City, a "city" of about 3,000 people. I was living in a ghost town, what used to be French Corral. It was the home of the first long-distance telephone line and was, during the gold rush era, a bustling little place. By the time I got there, bustling had long since ceased. I settled in for a summer of writing, reading, and running.

I've heard that people sometimes, when finishing a hard race like a marathon, will burst into tears. I've never experienced that rush of emotions after one of my own races. Sure, I can be tired, or disappointed, or elated, even (though rarely) with my times. The first time I choked up with emotion after a race was at a race I hadn't entered, and hadn't even run.

Ralph, a running buddy from North Carolina, was running the Western States 100-mile trail race. Since I was going to be spending the summer in the backyard of the race, I volunteered to "pace" Ralph the last 20 miles of the race. Pacing an ultra is a contradiction in terms. Pace, when you're going in and out of two thousand–foot canyons, on a single-track trail, isn't exactly the right word for the speed at which you are moving through space. In most 100-mile races, runners may be accompanied for the last section. It's not so much to help them finish in a certain time, though that may be part of the objective. More that it can be dangerous for runners to be out alone at night, on a remote trail, after full day of pushing themselves. The risks of falls, dehydration, disorientation, and just plain stopping and going to sleep under a tree are mitigated by the presence of another person.

At Western States, pacers are allowed from Foresthill, at mile 62, to the finish. Most runners have two people run with them for the last portion. It's the easiest section of the race—relatively flat, although in the foothills of the northern California Sierra, flat is always a relative term. Typically, a runner will have one pacer from Foresthill to Green Gate, at mile 80. A second pacer will accompany the runner to the finish. For the final mile and half, friends and family can join in.

I was to pace Ralph in from Green Gate. Actually, I was going to jog down the steep 2 miles from the Green Gate aid station to meet him after he'd crossed the river. It's not a trivial thing, crossing that river. Especially after 80 miles, especially in the dead of night, when it's cold and the water is icy and deep. No way was I going to cross that river. Our friend George was planning to run with Ralph from Foresthill to the river crossing, but George had moved to a new city and begun a new job and had to bail out. No problem, said Ralph, he'd run to Green Gate alone and then I'd pick him up and finish with him.

I got to Foresthill in the afternoon and spent it watching the show. The aid station is set up outside the Foresthill Elementary School, in a teeny tiny town that once a year teems with runners, pacers, and crew members. I'd met a number of the ultrarunning big dogs during my summer stay and chatted happily with them, awaiting reports of the leaders from previous check points in the race. They began coming through at around 4 p.m., the leaders, looking astonishingly fresh even after 62 brutal miles.

While the winners will run the 100 miles in around sixteen hours, the big deal at Western States is to finish in under twenty-four. That gets you a silver belt buckle. In order to complete the race officially and earn your brass buckle, you must finish in under thirty hours. Ralph, a sub-three-hour marathoner, was planning merely to enjoy the experience—he didn't care about going under twenty-four, just wanted to finish. An engineer by training, he had e-mailed me a spreadsheet of his anticipated arrival at each of the aid stations. He was planning to be at Foresthill at 8:24 p.m. He had a crew of thousands—family members from both coasts who would be helping him along the way. I didn't know any of them, and so I wore my number—his number, our number—on my shorts as I milled around Foresthill.

A man and boy bounded up and asked if I was me. I had just met a portion of Ralph's crew. His girlfriend, Cindy, and her two girls, his son and daughter, his brother and sister-in-law gathered around. They told me that Ralph announced, the last time they'd seen him at Michigan Bluff at mile 55.7, that he wanted a pacer in from Foresthill.

"No problem," I said, and we walked over to Pacer Central, where the pacers sign in and where folks wanting to volunteer to pace registered. Most want to pace runners who will be coming in under twenty-four hours; by the time we got to Pacer Central, we were told that there was no one available.

"Why don't you do it?" asked the nice man volunteering at Pacer Central. I told him that I was doing it—from Green Gate on in. "Why don't you run the whole way?"

Yeah, right. Easy for you to say. "I can't run that far," I told the nice but persistent man at Pacer Central.

"Yes you can," he said, knowing nothing about me. "It'll be slow."

After a small hissy fit, I said I'd try it. We decided that if I pooped out, Ralph's brother, Paul, could run the last 7 miles with him, and I could drop at the Highway 49 aid station.

I rushed to change into my running clothes and regretted having downed a gigantic "Navajo" taco only twenty minutes before. I can eat this, I'd thought, since I won't even start running until after 1 a.m.

Ralph came into Foresthill at around five minutes to nine. He looked good. He slurped down a can of pineapple chunks, ate some grapes, and, just after 9 p.m. on Saturday night, as it was beginning to get dark, we took off running.

We chat, we catch up. Ralph asks about my summer. I talk about the writing I've not been doing, but all the running I have. I tell him about my most recent race, a tiny trail marathon near where I've been living. I won the women's race—first out of about five women, eighth overall. He talks a bit about his training, about how the race has been going for him so far. There was snow in the early miles and ungodly heat in the canyons. He talks about spending time with his new girlfriend, Cindy, her daughters, and his kids.

I'm loving running at night. I run behind him, shining my flashlight on his feet. How beautiful is this? I ask. How fortunate are we to be out here? Even after 65 miles, Ralph agrees. As we run down a long fire road we look up at the stars.

"Do you know your constellations?" he asks.

I do not.

"That's Scorpio," he says, "and wow, look at the Milky Way tonight."

He hits a rock and catches a toe.

"Ralph," I say. "Don't look at the stars now. Stay focused, keep running."

We get to an aid station. The volunteers grab our bottles and fill them for us. I ask what he wants to eat. Ralph has been suffering from nausea since Foresthill.

"Just grapes," he says. He eats a couple, a piece of potato with salt, but he's not happy. His stomach is bothering him.

"Here," I say, "try a saltine." Sick food. He eats it. I offer another to him and hold my breath. He takes it, eats it. I stuff a bunch of saltines into the pocket of his shorts. He thanks the volunteers. Often curmudgeonly, I was expecting Ralph to be a little grouchy by this point. He has not been. I'd been warned by ultra-veteran friends: What happens on the trail, stays on the trail. If he yells at you or gets angry, don't take it personally. I've also been told that you see people's truest selves come out during these kinds of events. Ralph has been sweet, and gracious, and kind.

"I'm sorry," he says, as we walk out of the aid station. "I know this is runnable, but I need to let my stomach settle."

"Don't apologize to me," I tell him. "This is your race. Your event," I say. "I'm along for the ride."

We run slowly, walking the inclines, in comfortable silence. Sometimes we talk. At the next aid station he is feeling worse and doesn't want to eat. He wants to sit down. He does.

"Okay," I tell him after a minute or two. "That's it. We need to get going now. Can you eat anything?"

He shakes me off.

"Come on, Ralph."

He gets up. We move out again.

His stomach is bothering him. "You look strong," I tell him. "You're running smoothly."

"Thank you," he says.

We get to the aid station on the near side of the river crossing. Ralph's weight is down. The day before the race all the runners are weighed and the number is written on a bracelet. Throughout the race, their weight is monitored. If they lose more than 7 percent of their body weight, the bracelet will be cut off and they will be pulled from the race and rehydrated. A weight gain can signal hyponatremia, a dangerous condition where blood sodium gets too low. This is not the kind of running you do for your health.

The medical volunteers ask Ralph to stay, to sit for about fifteen minutes. They check his blood pressure and pulse. I bring him cups of grapes, and a few potato slices. He takes them, but doesn't eat. I bring him a cup of hot soup. He takes a sip and gives me back the cup.

Finally he's good to go. Only now we have to cross the river. It is two o'clock in the morning. While it's not very cold out, it's not warm either. The water is wide. And cold. And deep. A sturdy cable has been strung across, and there are volunteers planted mid-stream to help us out. Still, the footing is difficult and getting wet with 20 miles still to go sucks, no matter how you look at it. This is the part I did not want to do. I really did not want to do this part. I start in. This is Ralph's race. The closest I get to complaining is to lament, not for the first time in my life, that I wish I were taller. The water comes up to my rib cage.

We make it across and are met by Paul and Roz, Ralph's brother and sister-in-law. We wrap a blanket around Ralph and sit him down. He is shivering. They take off his shoes and replace them with a dry pair. I go to get him some more saltines and some hot chocolate. I towel off quickly, shaking myself like a wet horse, and begin to shiver. Roz gives me her jacket.

I start to tell Ralph that it's time to get moving again. He looks up at me with a glare that makes my stomach hurt. He says nothing.

"Come on, Ralph," I say. "We've gotta go."

He says nothing. We wait a few more minutes, and then he gets up.

We walk the hard 2-mile climb up the fire road from the river crossing to the Green Gate aid station. Cindy meets us at the top. The kids are sleeping in the van somewhere. Ralph sits. Cindy tends to him, and I eat a handful of peanut M&Ms. I put on another shirt, and we load up with fresh flashlights. I eat two more big handfuls of peanut M&Ms, a couple of quarters of sandwiches—if I don't keep myself strong, I won't be much good to Ralph—and tell him it's time to go.

"This is a nice easy downhill stretch," I say.

This is the part of the course I've already run. This is the part I was planning to run with him, and I've done my homework. I know where the aid stations are and have a good idea of the terrain.

"This is pretty runnable," I say. "You wanna run?"

"No."

A few minutes later he begins to run.

"You're looking real strong and smooth." I am not lying. That will come later.

We approach other runners and their pacers. It's not hard to tell who has which role. The pacers, many of them women, are happy and peppy. The runners are usually silent. "Looking good," we pacers say to the runners and to each other. The runners grunt thanks and carry on.

"How about a gel," I ask.

"No."

A few minutes later he takes a gel from his shorts. I help him get the water bottle out of his pack, he drinks, and hands it back to me. I stuff it back in his waist pack. We talk about how good our crew is, Paul and Roz. Cindy. We run.

"You're doing great, Ralph."

"Thanks. Thanks," he says, "for doing this for me. I really appreciate it." I can hear fullness in his voice.

"It's my pleasure," I tell him honestly.

"You doing okay?" he asks.

"Don't worry about me. I'm fine."

Soon we're at the Auburn Lake Trails aid station. There are big heaters going, and I stand in front of one while Ralph gets weighed again. His weight has remained fairly stable, though still down about eight pounds from the start. I get him some potato soup, but he can't eat it. I try to drink some, but find I don't want it either. I get him a handful of Wheat Thins, which he likes and eats.

For the past 15 or so miles Ralph has been focused on one thing. "You know what I really want," he says, periodically. To stop? To go to sleep? A steak?

What Ralph wants after 80 miles is red Hawaiian Punch.

"You're a weird guy."

"That's what I want," he says.

This portion of the trail has been marked by glowsticks, their eerie green light is a beacon for us. As we run along, Ralph slows.

"Are we on the course?"

"Yes," I say without a second's hesitation. I'm thinking to myself—*ohshitohshitohshit*—have I led him off the trail? I haven't been paying attention. I've been shining my flashlight on his feet, focusing on keeping him going and not even noticing the trail markers. We both know that I have a history of going off course during trail races.

"Are you sure we're on the course," he asks. "I haven't seen any trail markings for a while."

"Yep," I say, "we're fine."

My voice is completely confident, even a little dismissive of such a question.

"Just keep moving."

I'm dying inside, panicking, wondering what to do.

"Oh, yeah, you're right. There's a marker."

I give thanks to every deity I've ever heard of, and on we go.

In a while we can hear the music from Brown's Ravine—Brown's Bar the locals call it, since it is staffed by members of the Hash House

Harriers, a worldwide group that prides itself on its motto: A drinking club with a running problem. I've been told that because of the acoustics of the canyons, you can hear the music well before you are close to the aid station.

"Are we almost at the aid station?"

"No. Not for a while. Remember I warned you that we'd hear the music miles before we get there."

"Yeah."

Soon, though, we can hear the generator for the lights, and I begin to see patches of white ashy stuff on the ground and bizarre symbols that I vaguely wonder about: could they be related to some odd satanic ritual? Then I see the neon Coor's beer sign and remember that this is the Hasher's aid station—the flour and symbols are hashing culture.

We trundle in and the folks are rowdy. I suspect they've spent the night drinking. Ralph sits.

"Excuse me," I say, "but this is your lucky day."

He looks at me, dazed.

"What is it that you want?" I ask him.

Now he's looking confused and little cross. He's run 89.9 miles and is not in the mood for guessing games.

I point to the table next to him on which is sitting a big bottle of red Hawaiian Punch. He smiles as I pour him a cup.

"How often in life does that happen?" I ask.

This is the home stretch.

"It's time to go."

He struggles to his feet. It's beginning to get light. It's beautiful out here and I say so. Ralph mutters agreement.

"How far to the next aid station?"

"Not far." I can't remember, but I figure "not far" is the right answer.

"We'll go up a little and cross the highway to the aid station—we'll see our people there again—your people. Won't that be nice?"

Grunt.

After the aid station, there's a short uphill that's a bit nasty and rocky. Then it evens out and then we get to cruise down Cool canyon—it's a nice stretch, I tell him. I've done that part a couple of times.

"You'll like it, Ralph."

He grunts.

Apparently someone once asked Ann Trason—the long-reigning queen of ultradistance running, the woman who won this race eleven times, who always came in among the top ten men—if, at the end, she ran from aid station to aid station.

"No," she said. "Sometimes it's tree to tree."

I tell this to Ralph. I tell him, too, about a book, a good book about writing, called *Bird by Bird* by Anne Lamott. It gets its title from a story about the author's brother. He'd had a report due in school on birds. He'd left it, of course, to the last minute. Then it was crunch time and the task seemed overwhelming. When he asked his father, a writer, how he should approach it, the answer was simple: bird by bird.

I tell Ralph about a conversation I'd had with another runner, a guy like Ralph in his middle forties, but faster. A 5K, 10K kind of guy. I'd asked him how he gets through races, how he deals with the pain. He tells himself, he told me, that when he starts feeling badly, he reminds himself that as much as it hurts right now, in a little while he will feel better. You just need to make it through the hard part. Ralph is walking now. You will feel better, I tell him. Soon.

We reach the last major aid station, the Highway 49 crossing. He gets weighed. He's doing okay, not great. I tell him about a tee-shirt I saw while waiting around at Foresthill. On the front it said "Western States." On the back, "Lose 14 pounds in one day—ask me how!" Our crew is there. The kids are awake again. It's morning. We don't linger long.

We hammer down the canyon. After 31 miles of this, running and walking through the night, I'm getting a little tired. I am astonished as Ralph cruises down this canyon at seven, maybe seven and a half minutes per mile. Even as I keep up with him, I wonder how he has the strength, the legs, to do this now after what he's been through.

Soon, very soon, we are at the bottom, at No Hands Bridge—mile 96.8. Water bottle refills. Saltines. I eat more peanut M&Ms, though I feel I've had enough for a lifetime. Ralph goes through the misting shower that has been set up—it's getting warm again now that the sun is fully risen.

"The next part is a climb," I say, "but it's only a 3 percent incline." I'd heard this from someone, and she told me that she would be reminding her runner of the gentleness of the grade when she paced him in.

"We're practically done," I tell Ralph, as we start up the fire road that parallels the water.

"What river is that?"

"The North Fork of the American River." I have no idea what river it is. But at this point he'd rather hear definitive answers from me, even if they turn out to be not exactly correct. It was, I learned later, the Middle Fork. Oh well.

Eventually the trail goes up more steeply.

"Three percent grade?" Ralph snaps. This is the first tiny bit of pique he has shown.

"For the most part," I say. "Keep going. We're almost there."

We've been walking the whole way, though it is quite runnable. From the start Ralph was clear about his goal. He wanted only to finish. He reckoned it would take him twenty-seven and a half hours, but he didn't care if it took 29:59. No big difference to him; he just wanted to finish. At each aid station, there are times listed—the twenty-four-hour and thirty-hour cut-offs. We'd had a comfortable margin of one and a half to two hours the whole way. But somehow, I don't know, maybe it was the 93 miles of hard running, Ralph thought that we were dangerously close to not making it. That's why he charged so furiously down Cool canyon. Now he realizes that we have about three hours to cover the last 3 miles. He has no interest in doing anything other than walking it in.

We reach the end of the dirt trail and come to the last aid station, Robie Point. It is mile 98.9, and we are met by Roz and the four teenagers. They are allowed to join us for this last part of the race, now on the paved streets of Auburn. I jog ahead to chat with the girls, while Stewart, Ralph's thirteen-year-old son, stays back to check on his dad. So many hours ago, as we were leaving Foresthill, at the beginning of my run with Ralph, I heard Stewart call out to him: "I love you, Dad."

An older woman is walking her dog.

"You're almost there," she says to us. "You've got one little uphill left—and then you'll go down. Do you need some water?" Western States is the Boston Marathon of ultrarunning—not just because you have to qualify to get in, but because it too offers knowledgeable, helpful, and local spectators.

At a house along the way, there's a small group of people hanging out, a couple of couples. "What's the number of your runner," they call out to me. "Number 404," I say. They consult a program. As Ralph walks past they cry out: "Ralph—all the way from North Carolina! You're looking great! Almost there! Good job!"

I am getting tired. I am sleep deprived, and I've been on my feet for a long time. But more, I am starting to feel emotionally shaky. I drop back and walk beside Ralph.

"Do you know," I ask, "who that was? Do you know who was cheering you on as you are finishing this race?"

"No."

"I'm pretty sure that was Karl Anderson and his wife, Ann Trason."

"Really?" He looks up. He smiles.

We come down the last hill, and Cindy is waiting for us.

"This is what's going to happen," Ralph says, sounding like his old, bossy self. "You're all going to be on the track with me, that last portion. We are all going to cross the finish line together. All of us." Cindy demurs, says she doesn't want to run. She wants to take a photograph of the finish.

"No," says Ralph. "We're all going to finish together."

We walk, a big pack.

Ralph and Cindy hold hands. I stay off to the side. Suddenly, I am overcome. My throat tightens. I clench my jaw. I am terrified that I am about to cry. This is not my race. I will not cry.

There are two chutes at the finish. Runners are directed through the one on the left, pacers and crew to the right. As Ralph cuts off to the finish line he looks dead at me and points. He points at me and says nothing. But I know. I know.

"Good job, Ralph," I say. My voice is cracking and I look away. I will not cry.

It's a few minutes after 10 a.m. We spent thirteen hours together. We spent the night together, and together we saw the sun come up. We ate, we drank, we peed on the trail. Burps, farts—there's no place for modesty. It's intimacy on a different level. Now it's over. Ralph did what he wanted to do, and I got to help him do it. Stewart, remembering, I think, my protestations of the night before, my saying that I couldn't run that far, comes over to me and tells me I did good. I will not cry. Ralph's mother thanks me. I hear Ralph telling Cindy what I've told him on the trail—that we had a most excellent crew and that I had said that Cindy had done an amazing job of holding everything together.

It's time for me to leave. I want to go home and go to sleep. I have a forty-minute drive to get back, horses to feed, a book to write.

As soon as I get in the car, I cry.

Injuries

17

Run long enough and you will be injured.

How you deal with injury depends, in large part, on who you are. Many of us try to deny our mortal coil. But we can't deny our mortal muscles, tendons, ligaments, and bones.

The entry-level damage used to be called "shin splints." They are a rite of passage, the beginning runner's introduction to the wide world of sports injuries, usually the result of enthusiasm: too much, too soon. Or running in bad shoes. Or having bad form (though running is forgiving of all sorts of form; one need only watch Olympic gold medalist Michael Johnson's odd body position to know that form and function can be divorced). They can come from running on hard surfaces, or on canted roads. Shin splints are pains in the shin. They are now called things like post tibial stress syndrome.

Treating them, though not as easy as pie, is often as easy as RICE, the fallback for all sorts of inflammations and injuries—Rest, Ice, Compression, Elevation. They can also be treated by building up and stretching supporting muscles—though the jury is out on the whole stretching thing. There are those who believe in it and those who don't. I don't. The one thing everyone seems to agree on is that if you're going to stretch, do it only once you've already warmed up the muscles. Jog for a mile or so and then, if you must, do your yoga moves, your reaching and bending, your calisthenics.

Shin splints can turn into stress fractures. Immediate diagnosis requires a bone scan; it takes a while for the thin line to show up on an x-ray. But often you don't need medical tools to know.

I can tell if I have a stress fracture by running my finger along the general area that is bothering me and listening for the part where I yelp. Stress fractures are point-specific. If you press on them, they will hurt. A lot. They require time off.

Pain on the outside of the knee is frequently the result of a tight ilio-tibial band, a ribbon-like sheath of fascia that connects the knee to the hip. It gets irritated and inflamed. Running with ilio-tibial band friction syndrome—ITBFS—is like having someone put a stick in your bicycle wheel. Especially on the downhills.

Once I so enraged my IT band that it took months to forgive me. But I refused to back down. Mike and I were going to his family's home for Christmas, and I thought it would be fun to do a midnight New Year's Eve run in Minneapolis. (Why I thought this is beyond me—I'd never before seen a minus sign in front of temperatures in the twenties.) The pain at the side of my knee wasn't getting any better, so I went to the Duke sports medicine clinic and explained my problem to the orthopedist. He injected a steroid into my bursa—the space under the kneecap. The shot hurt so much I threw up, just missing the doctor. But I went to Minnesota and ran the race. (It was very cold.) My IT band raged for another two months.

Ankle sprains are a danger if you run on uneven terrain. If you land badly enough, you will hear a crunch and within minutes your shoe will be too small. Do not take off this too-small shoe until you are home. In the middle of a trail run, it will serve to compress the injury. Besides, you won't get it back on. There is a great and understandable temptation to peek and see the colors change; they can be as showy and bright as autumn in New England. Twist one ankle enough, and it will be weakened and prone to twist again. I used to wear braces—I called them my polo wraps, like what you'd use in transporting a dear horse—during long and nasty trail races. People would ask if I had weights on my legs. I'd usually say yes. Better to appear tough and stupid than weak and twisted.

If the sprain is bad enough, you have to re-train the nerves. Standing on your damaged foot with arms outstretched and eyes closed will wake up the pathways of proprioception. It sounds and looks funny, but it helps.

There are so many ways the feet can go bad. The easiest is the lowly blister. If you are in the middle of a long race and have no hope of stopping or bandaging it, the pain can be catastrophic. Khalid Khannouchi had the chance to get the world record in the marathon in his first race as a naturalized U.S. citizen. But the rabbit went out too slow and set a pace that was uncomfortable and not natural for the man who would later become the fastest marathoner in the world. It forced Khalid to change his stride and gave him blisters. He had to drop out of his first race as an American.

Achilles was not the only one who had trouble with his heel. Plantar fasciitis has deprived me of many of my running partners. It's a sneaky pain—usually felt most strongly after rolling out of bed in the morning. Just when I started getting serious about running, and looked forward to joining my old pal Val on long trots, I lost her to sesamoiditis, a bad pain in the ball of her foot, near her big toe. It took years for her to get over it, during which she had to wear shoes that cost hundreds of dollars and worse, were ugly.

Running is not a regenerating kind of activity; it can even be eroding. You can wear down the cartilage in your knees. It's called chondromalacia. If there's a tracking problem with the knee cap, you can end up with patellafemoral syndrome. Both of these are more commonly known as "runner's knee."

My friend Reggie is an orthopedic surgeon. He has seen bazillions of injuries due to running. He once told me that when a runner comes in, he asks a question: "Do you run for your physical health or your mental health?" It makes a difference in how he approaches their care. With those who run for the latter reason, he says, he has to be more patient.

Most experienced runners know to back off as soon as they start to feel an injury coming on. They will rest, ice, and eat massive quantities of vitamin I—ibuprophen, or what I like to refer to as the "Breakfast of Champions." Backing off is hard to do. Most runners love to run, and become cranky and hard to live with when they can't. We lie to ourselves—*That pain isn't really there.* Or if we acknowledge that it is, *It isn't really* that *bad*—and keep going until it's too late.

Not being a cook, I rarely think about preparing food. But once I was given a good piece of advice about baking: It's done before you think it is, so take it out sooner rather than later. You could extrapolate that to running pains: Ease off before you think you need to.

Otherwise, cozy up to a good physical therapist.

Ultras

18

For years I drove a reminder of my first ultramarathon. I had gone to Charleston, West Virginia, to visit my brother and sister-in-law, and to run the Rattlesnake 50K. It was a Three Stooges kind of day—everything that could go wrong, did, starting with my not waking up on time, driving too fast to get to the race, careering off the road and popping a tire, thinking I was going to have to run to the start (but thankfully was picked up by another runner), getting into a political argument with a guy on the course and then straying off the course and adding a couple of miles, falling three times (including once on my head), and finishing messed up enough to win "Best Blood." My family was there at the finish, and my brother took care of my car while I scraped the blood and mud off of my pathetic self. It took him a very long time to attend to the car, and when he came back he was driving a vehicle that was not mine. "We decided to get you a new car," Mark said. This was the beginning of my life as an ultrarunner.

Mark called one day to say that he'd read in his local paper about a brand-new event—The Highlands Sky 40-Mile Trail Run—at a place where they skied in the winter and resorted in the fall: Canaan Valley.

I had visions of wandering lost for forty years, trying desperately to reach the promised land of a finish line forty miles away. Until I learned that in West Virginia, Canaan rhymes with inane.

If you rent a big house, I told my brother, we could all go up and I could run the race. (This is the same brother who, when I told him that I had bought a black leather jacket and needed a motorcycle to accessorize it—ha ha—got me a Honda Rebel 250cc.) Within a nano-second, Mark had rented a big house, and I was compelled to enter a race longer than I had ever run.

My sister-in-law comes from hardy Virginia stock. Her family history is straight Southern Gothic. One day I will tell their stories and no one will believe it is anything other than fiction. The four sisters, three of whom now live in Charleston, are close and tolerant. Except that they do not tolerate whining, from each other or from others. When we decided that my brother, his eight-months' pregnant wife, two of her sisters, one five-year-old child, my sixteen-year-old dog, Hannah, and her two canine cousins would accompany me to this race, they said I would be allowed an hour of whining, no more. The quarters were too close, the drive too long. I was lucky to get an hour, they said.

But, but, but, I said. I've never run that far. I don't know if I can do it. It's up a mountain and back down. It's the first year of the race—things always go wrong the first year. I could get lost. I often get lost. It's desolate and deserted up there. There are no previous times to try to gauge how long it will take. It could be wet. It could be cold. (I am always cold.) I will fall. (I always fall.) There might not be enough—or the right kind of—food at the aid stations. I haven't trained enough. I'm scared.

You have forty-seven minutes of whining left, they said.

After the pre-race briefing, I thought I was going to have to plead for more time. Dan Lehmann, the race director, casually mentioned that there were cables across some of the deeper, trickier stream cross-ings. He emphasized the rockiness of the course. He noted that it had been a rainy spring and that the peat moss sods were, well, sodden. The weather up there, a freak of nature kind of place, atypically bare and barren for lush West Virginia, was highly changeable. It could be cold. Windy. You will get muddy, he said. There's a hose at the finish, he said.

I do not like stream crossings. I do not like being cold. I do not like losing my shoes in the mud. I don't even like point-to-point races. Except, of course, for the Boston Marathon. As in Boston, we filed onto buses. At Highlands Sky we loaded at 5:00 a.m. to get to the start. We drove until it was light, and then, as in Boston, waited in line for the porta-potties. At 6:00 a.m., Dan said, not terribly loudly, "Okay, go ahead, have fun," and we went ahead.

In the first few miles, I started a conversation with a guy my brother, a lawyer, had pointed out the day before at race registration. He does constitutional law, Mark had said. I trotted up and asked the long-haired young man what kind of constitutional law issues arose in Charleston, West Virginia. Lots, it turned out.

A number of us listened while making the first big climb. Con Law Man talked about defending a student who wanted to start an anarchy club in a local high school (the irony of forming an anarchy club seemed to get lost somehow), defending the KKK, and suing the state legislature. We joked about how the state prosecutor was being prosecuted for sexual harassment ("It's just how we talk to each other in this office," was his defense), and that the governor's love-letter e-mails to his mistress had recently been published in the newspaper. What kind of a state is this, I asked? One like any other, Con Law Man said. I guess. Then, as usual in ultras, talk turned to other races, other towns. As we climbed higher, we spoke less and spaced out.

After a long, steep, rocky downhill, a woman I'd passed caught up and commended me on my downhill running. Short legs and fearlessness, I said, go a long way.

I asked about her running history and she told me that she'd run five 100-mile races, winning or coming in second. I apologized for not recognizing her name. Most people know my name, she said, because of last year's Vermont 100-mile race. Michele told me that she'd crossed the finish line and went straight into a coma for five days, suffering from hyponatremia. For years we heard about the dangers of dehydration, but hyponatremia has become a much bigger problem as more people are running for longer stretches of time. The advice to drink early and often has been superceded by warnings about the dangers of drinking too much water and washing the sodium out of your body. I thought about trying to take in more salt after that, and filled my bottles with electrolyte drink at the aid stations.

We were running in creek beds, through water and on jagged rocks. The first half was billed as the hard part; after mile 19 or so, it was supposed to be easy. Maybe, if running 7.3 miles on a straight dirt road, where all you see stretching ahead is uphill miles and ant-sized fellow runners, can be considered easy. Maybe, if running for hours through bogs of standing water and knee-deep, shoe-sucking mud can be considered easy. Maybe, if climbing to the top of a mountain ridge on rocks as big as basketballs and being buffeted by a strong wind can be considered easy. Maybe, if you don't think running 40 miles is a tough way to spend a day.

I crossed the line. That was hard, I said to Dan. I was smiling. It was hard. He said I looked fresh, happy. I was happy. How could I not be happy? The course was so well marked that even I would have had to work to get lost. The aid stations were not only well stocked, but well staffed. The volunteers were personal pit-crew for each runner, suggesting things that you didn't even know you wanted until they offered. The course was not only beautiful, but varied; something for everyone to love, and very little not to like (though the 7.3 miles of road was less than lovable).

That night, even though I should have known better, I ended up soaking in the hot tub. The sisters said I had a lot of whining time left, that I should feel free to let loose. But I could produce no whines, just kept smiling, feeling fortunate to be able to do something so wonderful, surrounded and supported by friends and family. It's hard to whine once you've arrived in the land of milk and honey.

I like to plan trips to visit family and friends around local races. Upstate New York, where my parents live, is known to historians as the "Burned Over District" for all the sects and religions that were founded there. It's where Joseph Smith was visited by the angel Moroni. It's where the Shakers did their quaking, where the Oneida Community practiced vegetarianism, group marriage, and sex without ejaculation. It's also where the Finger Lakes Runners Club currently puts on a plethora of trail races. I can usually find a race when I'm there, and I've been there enough that I have friends to do long runs with.

But I also like to take road trips by myself, going to new places, staying in hotels or camping overnight, seeing people I've met at other races and meeting new ones. I'm not afraid to travel on my own, and I'm good at starting conversations with strangers. I flirted through 20 miles of my first 50 miler.

At the start of the Mountain Masochist, I met a guy. We chatted for the predawn miles. When it got light, I saw that he was tall, dark, and handsome. And smart and funny. And he had more stories than I and shared them freely and gosh, for 20 miles it was like being on the world's best first date. Eric had bagged the international age group record in his first marathon: 2:48. At age eleven. He repeated at age twelve. Then he went to Harvard to row crew. He got an MBA from Wharton and now was training for an Ironman. I wanted to marry him.

He was starting slow and finishing strong, so he left me after 20 heart-fluttering miles. But a woman had caught up to me just as Eric took off. She said she'd heard someone call me by my name, said that she'd seen that I was entered and had been hoping to meet me. Hoping to meet me? Turns out, she'd read everything I'd written—both about running and higher education—and went on to say such nice things about my work that I felt like I could have run for days, fueled by the fluffing. Turns out, Sophie was as smart and funny as my boy Eric, and we had a grand time together.

When I reached the finish line, having taken it easy and met great new friends, David Horton, the race director greeted me. He said, "Rachel,

I gave you that low number. Why did you run so slow?" Indeed, I had messed things up for him. The first five women finished in the order he had seeded them. It would not be the only time I disappointed a race director.

I loved *I Love Lucy*. I loved Lucy. And you know what? Some days are Lucy days. Nothing goes right, you get yourself into messes, you get all dirty, other people find humor in your situation, and eventually everything works out. Desi comes home none the wiser for your adventures and mishaps and kisses you on the head.

I had moved to Montana and was excited to be able to explore by traveling to an ultra, a 50K, my favorite distance. I'd heard great things about the race (the course was beautiful) and not such great things (the race was poorly organized). But I was ready to race, ready to roll, and roll out of bed at 3:30 a.m. I did, giving myself plenty of time to cover the hour and half drive to make a 7 a.m. start.

There aren't many roads in the sparsely populated West. That I was able to get lost—truly, deeply, 30 miles-out-of-the-way-headed-north-instead-of-south lost—is a tribute to how poor my sense of direction is. It was an achievement, of sorts. As I drove through a maze of voluptuous mountains and rocky, shale-showered hills, I noticed the natural beauty even as I swore at the clock in my car, the illumination of the digits becoming less sharp as the sun rose and I realized that there was no way, even once I'd turned myself around, that I could make it to the start of the race on time.

I did not. The Web site had directed me, without pretense of giving real directions, to something called "Legal Tender." I didn't have a clue what Legal Tender was, other than in some vague financial sense. Turns out, Legal Tender is a bar. The bar, when I found it, was closed (it was just past seven in the morning; I was not unhappy to see that bars were closed at this hour), and there was no indication that an ultramarathon had ever begun there.

I found a guy wandering around the parking lot and asked if he'd

seen a pack of wan and weedy runners go by. "Yeah," he said, from be-
neath a dirty baseball cap. "They ran under the interstate and along the
frontage road." I drove until I found a familiar herd, laden with water
bottles and fanny packs, talking and laughing as they jogged along the
paved road. I pulled my car up close, perhaps too close, to a barbed wire
fence on the side of the road and jumped out. I took mental stock: I
made sure that a number of women had already passed by, I tightened
the laces on my trail shoes, and I started running.

The paved road gave way to dirt, and what had been, at first, rolling
hills became one long ascent, an unremitting climb. Wide and rutty,
the road climbed—we climbed—beside pastures etched into the sides
of mountains. I ran easily. Since I had missed the race, this would be,
for me, just a run. I wanted to enjoy it.

It was a long way to the first aid station. When I got there I accosted
the volunteers and explained my situation: I had arrived late to the start
and hadn't been able to register. Because the entry fee was uncharacter-
istically steep for this kind of event, I'd decided not to enter in advance,
assuming, since nothing was said on the Web site, that I would be able
to sign my forms and fork over my money on race day.

As I've said, I do not approve of bandits. I don't believe in taking
part in an event without having paid for goods and services, and, having survived the headache of being on organizing committees, I know
the importance of having runners sign waivers indemnifying the race
and the race directors. I reckoned that in such a small race—there
were only thirty people in the 50K and another thirty in the 100K—I
would be able to settle up with the race director at the finish. But I
knew, too, that the volunteers on the course would have to account for
me. I gave them my name and told them that I wanted to sign a proxy
for the race waiver. I was assured by friendly aid station workers that
they would call ahead to the race director and let her know that I was
on the course, and I was sent on my way.

Each time I passed a woman, I alerted her to the fact that I wasn't
racing. I'd come up to her, say hello, and explain that I didn't have a

number, I wasn't racing. Even those who acted like they didn't think of themselves as competitive knew exactly where in the group of women they stood. Women say they just want to finish. Women say they just want to have a good time. Women do not say to each other: "I'm here to win, to kick your ass and break the course record. And then, after the race, I want to have a beer with you."

I settled in behind Dana, running in third place, who, I learned, had been coming here with her dad since she was a teenager. Now, at twenty-six, she was running it for the sixth time, in the company of her husband Rino, just ahead. Her dad was behind. They were part of a contingent of Canadians who came each year for this tiny little race, giving it a family reunion atmosphere.

We chatted and then I couldn't help it: I started laughing. Who says that ultras are without spectator support? While we ran, we were watched—and I want to believe, no, I do believe, cheered—by a number of strong and sturdy cows with whom we were clearly, and in slippery, stinky, tell-tale fashion, sharing the trail. They watched as we passed, and we heard them mooing, calling, cheering.

We ran on single track through an area that had been decimated by fire. It was eerie and beautiful, a cliché of the cycle of life: ravaged trees, tall skeletons, stood anorexic, while their chubby little sisters, fresh and green, grew up among them.

Dana started to fade and urged me to go on ahead. I picked up my pace and continued climbing to arrive at an aid station at the top of the mountain staffed by men who were clearly runners, huddled around a campfire. I launched into my windy explanation—missed the start, will sign a waiver—and they stopped me. They didn't care if I'd registered; they just wanted to know what they could get for me. Water? Electrolytes? Cookies? Pretzels? What do you need? What can we give you? This is why I like racing.

What I knew about the course is that from there it went down 3 miles to another aid station. Then you had to turn around and come right back. That makes for hard running, flying down steep slopes knowing that soon you will be slogging back up. But out-and-backs provide a welcome opportunity to take a measure of the race: I watched the leaders, tall young men, with legs long and strong, as they powered up the hill I was pounding down. I saw the first-and second-place women. Saw the look in their eyes when they realized I was there—recognized that look from my own racing—and soothed and smoothed by explanation and assurances.

At the turnaround I did my song and dance for the volunteers. "How did you get lost?" they asked, knowing that the start of the race was within spitting distance of the exit off the interstate. They smiled and told me I was doing well. I asked for salt tablets and grabbed a handful of mini-Butterfingers and some animal crackers and left them shaking their heads at my lack of directional ability.

I climbed, eating my cookies, biting off the heads first, the way you have to when you're eating food in the shapes of animals, trying to shake out of my head the song that had been with me for the last 15 miles—Dave Matthews, "The Space Between." It wasn't unpleasant going back up, not at all. I ran and then walked, the way we ultrarunners do, walking with a purpose, with vigor, and then running again.

I began to smell the campfire and was greeted by the sound of my own name coming from the voices of the handsome running men. I was back. I loved this aid station and had thought, more than once, on the way back up about how happy I would be to pass by there again. It had everything a runner could want: candy, Canadian whiskey, and hot men. But when I got to the summit, all I wanted was oxygen—more ambient oxygen.

Pushing down the hill I caught the second woman, Jackie, a local runner. She'd been running with a guy, but we soon lost him, picking up the pace while we told each other our stories, our lives, the way women do. She was a mother and snuck in her training where she could. I allowed as how there should be a separate division in races for women with children—I know well, though only from observation, the weariness of working mothers. Jackie was doing the 50K instead of the 100K this year, and was starting to flag. She told me that the woman ahead was, like us, in her forties, and that she was a strong runner. Jackie told me she always came in second in the race, second in the age division. She didn't want to get passed, but she knew she couldn't win.

"Go on ahead," she said to me, apologizing for walking an uphill. I thought about it for a nanosecond and said something like: "If you want to be alone, I will go ahead. But I'm not here to race and it's nice to have the company. If it would help you to have me here, to run in with you, I'll stay." She didn't have to think about it, so neither did I. We continued, talking about how many miles we had left, how long she thought it would take her, and what her best time for the course was. I was back in the position where I am most comfortable—pacing; not thinking about my own race, not racing, but helping someone do her best.

The last mile and half was on a dirt road. I began to look over my shoulder, not wanting Jackie to be passed near the finish. I ran in front, pulling her in my wake. We talked less and crossed the line—she crossed the line, I stepped to the side—in a time that bettered her personal best by thirteen minutes. It had been a good day.

I explained my plight, for the sixth time, to the man at the finish. He was co–race director, with his wife. He shrugged and said okay. I went off to see what there was to eat.

There was a small fire, and a huddle of runners stood around it, shifting tired weight from side to side, allowing fatigued muscles to rest. Jackie had already related my story of getting lost en route to the race and folks congratulated me on my effort, speculating on how I would have done if I'd actually arrived on time. I soaked up the attention—I do soak up attention—recounting my *I Love Lucy* adventure to get to the start (complete with a cop flashing his scary lights from across the other side of the—thankfully—divided highway) to a bunch of people I hoped would become friends. It was a small group, a good community, a reminder of why I love so much to go to races.

Foregoing harshly fried chicken and fluorescent potato salad that came from a milk carton, I looked around for something to eat. Someone pulled out a bag of marshmallows, graham crackers, Hershey bars, and I ran to get a stick. I impaled a gooey, gummy marshmallow on my spear, stood close to the warmth of the fire, and prepared to be really happy.

A voice boomed, asking for me. I looked up from my marshmallow. A woman, barrel-shaped on skinny legs, marched me away from the crowd and started in. She didn't introduce herself; I was left to assume that she was the race director. Her anger flashed: How dare I? What was I thinking? Why had I run the race without paying my entry fee? Who did I think I was? Oh dear. What would Lucy do? I looked for a rock to crawl under. I tried not to make funny faces. I made the easy decision to tell the truth.

In fact, I explained to the woman who looked at me like I was a dog who had gotten into the garbage, I had e-mailed her earlier in the week, asking for directions to the start (I know well my weaknesses) and telling her I was planning to cover the race for a national running magazine. I never heard back. I apologized 578 times and gave her an account of my attempts to make it okay (her aid station volunteers backed me up on my insistence on signing my name). Her ire was unquenchable. How dare I run without registering? I told her that since the Web site didn't say "No race day registration," I assumed it would be possible to do so in the ample amount of time I'd left myself to get there in the morning. I screwed up. I apologized again.

Finally, we got to the heart of the matter: money. She wanted the $100 check I had in my car. Of course, I said, I would give it to her—once I got back to my car (the start was about 14 miles from the finish—and in fact, I wasn't entirely sure where my car was). I said I'd mail it. She sneered. She growled.

I slunk back to the fire and was once again taken into the huddle; we went back to doing what runners do after races: talking about what we were running next. Jackie gave me a lift back to my car, and we spoke about mutual friends—even after such a short time living in a new home, entering the company of ultrarunners had given me a set of friends. I thought about the totality of my race experience. Yeah, it was a drag not making it to the start. Yeah, it was belittling to be yelled at like a child, a breach of the sense of community that is a large part of the reason we all go to these nutty, out-of-the-way races.

Finally, I thought about Lucy. Lucy always made it through. She believed in the basic goodness of people and that no matter how zany the situation you got yourself into, it would, in the end, all work out.

In the end, it all worked out.

The next year, I went back and ran the 50-mile race there. I made it to the start without getting lost, and I finished with an official number. The mean old race director had retired. Ding dong.

The Watch

19

A few years ago a colleague looked me up and down, taking in my sleek little black dress, my high-heeled boots, my diamond earrings. Then she allowed her eyes to light on my scrawny wrist. "That's a big watch for a little girl," she said to me.

It is a big watch.

It is my favorite thing.

I have two good watches—expensive, elegant watches. I have not worn them since I started running.

Since I started running, I have always worn a running watch. No matter where I am or how I'm dressed.

The first was a Timex Ironman. It was the ladies' version. It did not last long. I liked it well enough. I liked the fact that I could store my mile splits and then read them back to the friends who loved me well enough to listen to them. But it was too small.

So I gave it to a male friend, another runner, who, like me, had tiny wrists and big thighs. It fit him, he said, perfectly. And I got myself the men's version. This one I loved. Fluidity in gender roles and expectations can be a boon.

I'd lived through the Madonna-ed eighties, had worn zillions of heavy bangles on my arms and walked like an Egyptian. I was okay with hefty jewelry. But this watch—black, plastic, ugly (there was no denying that it was ugly)—was not jewelry. It was more like wearing underwear; I felt naked without it.

I can run without a watch, but I don't like to. I need to know how long I've gone, if not how far. If I decide to run for an hour, I want to know when it is time to turn for home. I don't like looking down and realizing that I've only been running for eleven minutes, when it feels like I've been out for miles already, but it is reassuring to know. I fetishize information.

In marathons, I toggle the display so that each mile split is big and the total elapsed time is little. This way, I have only to run for seven and a half or eight minutes at a time (or nine—whatever). I don't have to think of how many more miles—or hours—I have left. Just eight-odd-minute chunks. Afterward, I can replay the whole race just by looking at the times. Oh, there I go—too fast at the start. Oops: pee break. The fast, flat section. The uphill. The smell-of-the-barn sprint to the finish. It is so much more manageable to have to run only a mile at a time, rather than 26.2.

For years I wore my men's Ironman watches. Then I got a fancy Polar wrist-top computer. It has a pod that attaches to my shoe. It transmits to my watch my elapsed time; split time; pace; altitude; ascent; calories burned; minimum, maximum, and average speeds; and mileage. It practically tells me what to eat, when to speak, and who I should date. I wish it would learn to make coffee or take out the garbage.

This watch is even bigger than the Timex. It lodges on my wrist like a tumor. It calls attention to itself, though I keep it silent. It would ring and beep, if I allowed it to. My students love to tease me about it. "Nice watch," they say, using a literary device that I hope they could name. "Could you have found something a little bigger?"

I am rubber, you are glue, I say. I smile and tell them that I love my watch.

The numbers are huge. In the last year I have had to break down and buy drugstore reading glasses. I catch myself in dim restaurants thinking that my arms are not long enough to be able to read the menu. I need these big numbers. In races, I have to be able to see my time.

Often, in fact, I need to know the time. How many more pages of a book can I read before I have to leave for work? Why is he late? He should have been here seventeen minutes ago? You can measure out your life in coffee spoons, or by watching electrons dance across a small sheet of plastic.

One of the most tired complaints of daily life is not having enough time. We talk about being slaves to the clock. But my watch is a tool, an aid, not a master. I have learned, as do most trail runners, to measure my outings not in miles but in minutes, or often, in hours. As long as I have my watch, I know how long my run should be, no matter where I am—out for some number of minutes, and then back.

I know it looks silly on my slight wrist, this big watch. I am old enough to be comfortable looking silly. But I know something else. I know that it makes me look like a runner.

I have never cottoned to the idea of advertising what I do. No jewelry that says 26.2, no "On-On" bumper stickers to let others know that I, too, have taken part in the worldwide phenomenon of the Hash House Harriers. I rarely wear race tee-shirts, mostly because they are usually too big and not flattering. I don't wear my running shoes with civilian clothing.

There are no markers for me of the fact that I am a runner, except for the ways in which running has sculpted my body and this big eyesore of a watch. I know, when I see other people wearing watches like mine (well, like mine but usually smaller), that they are probably runners. I like to think of it as a secret handshake, a Masonic symbol; like the *ichthys*, the fish the early Christians drew in the dirt; it is a shibboleth, a password. I announce myself to fellow runners in a way that only they will recognize. I don't need to proclaim to the world that I am a runner, but I like to be distinguished by my peers.

I love my watch. It has many functions.

20

The Coach

This is how it happened: Because I wrote a running column for the local newspaper, I got an e-mail from the athletic director of Durham's North Carolina School of Science and Math, a boarding school for eleventh and twelfth graders, tuition-free for those who tested well enough to be admitted. Would I be interested in coaching cross-county for them?

I didn't know anything about cross-country—not how long the races were, or how meets were scored, or how many members were on a team. It was a team sport, wasn't it? I was spending my mornings writing, and then, when my head hurt from thinking too hard, I'd lie in bed all afternoon and read trashy mystery novels. This gig, I thought, might be a more productive way to spend my post-writing time.

I met with the athletic director. I told her I had no experience coaching, or even running, cross-country. I had taught the alphabet of standardized tests—SAT, MCAT, LSAT, GMAT, and GRE classes—and had, therefore, some limited teaching experience. Did that translate? I had worked in undergraduate admissions at Duke and knew that I liked teenagers. My most relevant and important qualification, the thing that got me the job, was that I was available every afternoon.

My interview was at 11 a.m. I met with the team at 3 p.m. the same day. In other words, they were desperate for a coach.

I spent the intervening hours worrying. Would I have to deal with girls who had eating disorders and boys who were surly and disaffected? High school girls ran to keep the weight off; boys because they weren't good at sports. I worried that with their undeveloped bodies, they would get injured. I worried that I would not be able to devise appropriate workouts, that I wouldn't be a good disciplinarian. I worried that they would hate me.

I decided that I would run with them, and that the girls would run with the boys. We would be one team. There was only one girl who was relatively fast. The rest were doing it for fun—for the social contact, for a release from the pressure of living in an intense academic environment. As far as I could tell, the girls' body images were as healthy as their laughter. The boys, on the other hand, were more worrisome. The fastest boys cared the most about their weight, believing as runners often do, that to be lighter would mean being faster. They complained about the bad—fattening—food in the cafeteria and ran more miles than was likely good for them. Their identities were often too tightly wrapped around their running.

The girls' team pretty much sucked. They would forget to look at their times when they crossed the finish line and would have no idea how they had done. I loved them for this, and for the many ways they supported each other—and me. From the beginning of the season, the boys talked about winning the league championship. Nate, a lanky, soft-spoken senior, was my clear choice to be captain. He was the fastest guy on the team, though Lance, a junior full of brash confidence coated in Southern good manners, was catching up. Lance called me ma'am until I yelled at him to stop. They were all from the South, and the boys refused to call me by my first name; I surprised myself when I started turning when I heard "Hey Coach."

I would write in the mornings and then drive 2 miles to the school, a former hospital on the edge of Durham's business district. We'd meet in the gym and then go out for a warm-up—girls and boys. After a mile or so, the girls would stop me. "We need to stretch."

"Oh you whiny little babies," I'd say. But they wanted to stretch, so I let them.

From the first, I told them that I was more interested in their academic successes and that running should be an outlet for them. School would always take precedence over cross-country. I devised drills for them. We'd have vocabulary shuttles, where I'd pair them up and they'd have to learn SAT words together while running sprints. I'd call out for definitions in the middle of a run, and ask my runners to use the words in sentences. None of them was going to be getting a scholarship for their running, even the fastest boys. But they were all smart and clearly talented in science and math. I wanted them to be better than proficient with language. So that's what we worked on. We did, in a desultory way, train for running. We had fartlek workouts—running hard for a minute or so, and then easy, and then hard again. We went to the track occasionally and did quarters or 800s.

Practices went well. Afterward, we would retire to the wrestling room, a small, stinky place covered with a thick mat, and we would do yoga and crunches. Or rather, the girls would do yoga, and the fast boys and I would try, without grace or a trace of fluidity, to put ourselves into poses that were not allowed by our taut muscles. I loved that the slowest girls were the best at stretching; that they got to be expert at something and to help the rest of us with our wiry, intractable bodies.

The hard parts, for me, were the meets. I had to get them there. Piloting a bus when you are at best a mediocre driver and have fourteen teenagers making fun of you—whooping it up if you happen to drive over a little curb or so slowly that traffic builds up for miles—is a challenge. Fortunately, I had an assistant coach, Ary, a recent college grad, a sprinter who was solid and sweet and unflappable. He would take over when I needed help. He lived on campus, as a resident assistant, and knew the workings of the school. And he was willing to drive the bus.

One of the moms always brought home-baked treats to our meets. Lance's dad showed up regularly, taking time off from work to see his son win. But most of their families lived far enough away that the kids had to cheer for each other. They did. There was no sniping, no snarky comments. They bonded as a team. The juniors had only recently arrived at the school, and the seniors looked out for them.

It took me a long time to understand the way cross-country meets are scored. I never really got the tactics (even though I know it's not that complicated). I left strategy up to the fast boys, comfortable in abdicating that responsibility because I knew they would do the right thing for the team. The girls didn't care much, and except for the fastest girl, none of them even wanted to compete.

It was not that long ago, but I do not remember her name, the fastest girl. She was small and doughy. She was a lot faster than the others, though not so fast that she would be getting into college based on her times. For one meet, I suggested that she stick with the second fastest girl to pull her along, to teach her what it felt like to race.

The next day at practice her father tracked me down, his face raging red before he even began to spit out his words. He couldn't believe I was asking his daughter to sandbag a race. He couldn't believe I was suggesting that she forsake her own competition for a girl who clearly wasn't ever going to be any good. At that moment I felt sorry for every high school teacher and coach whose students' parents lived nearby; I realized how lucky I was to be working at a boarding school. I quickly backed off the proposal that she might want to help a teammate, understood that my idea flew in the face of the drive to win that is so integral a part of sports.

What the father didn't understand was how marginalized his daughter was on the team; she was always alone, even though she longed to fit in. I wanted her to feel a part of it, to have the gift of assisting someone else; my intentions had to do with helping his daughter with something other than her running.

I was not, this is to say, a good coach. I didn't give a hoot about winning. The boy's team, without much input from me, came in second place in the league, their best showing in many years. But I was more excited for them when they got scholarships to good colleges. I liked it when they ran well, but I loved it when they brought me their essays, when they wanted to talk about the books they were reading.

I know how much fun it is to win. I know how it can boost the ego, fluff the soul. I love to win. But what I wanted these kids to understand was that it won't last. That the construct is not, as I had once believed, either/or. Not that you're either an intellectual or an athlete, but both/and.

After the season was over I took a bunch of my kids to a local club race. Before it began, I asked them, please, to call me by my name. Why, Coach, they asked? Are you embarrassed by us? No, I wasn't. But, come on, I said. I'm not your coach anymore. We're here with my friends. Just act like my friends. Call me Rachel.

After the race, when my name was called to collect my prize—a giant chocolate bar that I was more than happy to share with my kids—they erupted in a roar: *Go Mom!*

The Fuel

21

The pantry is much like the closet. It is jammed with items peculiar to runners and other endurance athletes.

There are canisters of electrolyte powder, mostly unopened. I rarely use sports drinks, except for during the longest runs on the hottest days of summer. I have always preferred to eat my calories, choosing to drink water and chew some more substantive form of sustenance.

There are packages of different kinds of energy gels. I started with Gu, vanilla flavored. When I got sick of that, I switched to chocolate, a flavor reminiscent of cafeteria pudding. When I got sick of that, I tried orange, which elicited fond memories of baby aspirin. When I got sick of that, plain. Then they all started to taste like racing.

I branched out to other brands. Clif Shots, boasting organic and more healthful ingredients, provided an assortment of new flavors and novelty. I tend to care more about boredom than I do about ingredients.

There are some old Power Gels, which I like because they are bigger—more calories—than the others. Some have caffeine, others don't. A number of years ago I weaned myself off coffee so that I could deploy it when needed: either medicinally or recreationally. Toward the end of endurance races, a shot of caffeine can go a long way toward getting me home.

There are lots of bars. Complex carbohydrates for before races; high protein for after. Small ones for snacks; big ones for meals. The most palatable combine the two major food groups: chocolate and peanut butter. Some are almost delicious. In addition to the sporting goods lines—Clif Bar, PowerBar—I often buy "diet" brands, like Slim-Fast and Atkins. Sometimes I want more protein, sometimes less fat, sometimes a bit of fiber. I choose carefully according to what I'm going to be doing. The body can only convert food into glucose and then into glycogen. During long runs, sugar is your friend. Fat and protein are slow and physiologically expensive to metabolize. While running, you want to be efficient. But afterward, you need to rebuild, to replenish.

There are orphaned packages of jelly beans, different kinds of sports gum, and funny little tubes of honey—all given out at marathon expos and toted home. Clif Bar has come out with gummy squares—Shot Bloks—that are close enough to candy that eating them can be a treat. Finding a good way to carry them on the run, however, has yet to be worked out. I have taken to putting them in sandwich bags and stuffing them down my running bra. This does the job, but they are often warm and salty.

Marathons have clung to the tradition of carbo-loading pasta dinners, even though the idea of pre-race carbo-loading has passed out of fashion. The sports medicine science seems to change as quickly as the weather in New England and no longer does anyone think it makes sense to eat a big meal of spaghetti before a race. Sure, in the few days leading up to a long race, you can help yourself by increasing the proportion of carbohydrate and cutting back on fat and protein, but it's a recipe for gut-ache to chow down too heavily the night before a race. You want to go out feeling good, and light, and with an empty bowel. But since pasta is a cheap and easy way to feed thousands of people, you can hardly blame race organizers for sticking with it.

Like most women, I have a complicated relationship with food. Having been forbidden to eat candy as a child, I developed an adult sweet tooth that is insatiable and more than a little stunted. I will pass up dark, elegant chocolate in favor of kid candy—Tootsie Rolls, Bit-O-Honeys, and caramel Bullseyes. When I left North Carolina to move to Montana, where I knew no one and had no ex-boyfriends to cook for me, my nutritional state became precarious. I'd have Peanut M&Ms for breakfast, Cherry Garcia for lunch, and Oreos for dinner. Eating so many sweets took away my desire for real food, and I felt sick much of the time. I lost weight.

Nike's motto used to be "Just do it." My modus operandi seems to be, "Why just do it, when you can overdo it?" So I make rules for myself. A few years ago, as my New Year's resolution, I banned the eating of sweets. Once I stopped eating chocolate every day, it wasn't hard to stay away from it. I had to find other ways to get my calories and turned to nuts, meats, cheese, and other, nutritionally dense foods. I was running better and didn't miss that feeling of eating one too many pieces of candy corn and then going over the edge.

The next year I decided to keep up with my abstinence, but amended it. I would not eat treats except on national holidays, defined by me to include my birthday, Valentine's Day, and Halloween, which are too candy-centric to miss. This worked well. On those days I collected and ingested such disgusting amounts of non-food that it was no stretch not to look at a Reese's Peanut Butter Cup again for another month.

But then, during an ultra, I realized I needed yet another amendment. The best way to get quick and easy calories during a race is to eat candy or cookies. Race organizers know this, and ultras all over the country often have aid-station buffets that are McDonald's-like in their uniformity: M&Ms, Chips Ahoy, Oreos, Fig Newtons, and gummy bears. No matter where you're racing, you'll find these staples. Many races also have volunteers who will bake brownies or cookies.

While I always intend to take it easy and to eat my way through the miles, when I'm in the middle of a 50K or longer race, I never want to stop and savor the goodies. But I do need the fuel. So the rule became: treats on national holidays (my version) and days when I run 26.2 miles or longer.

This is better in theory than in practice. In theory I look forward to marathons or ultras because I will be able to eat sweets. The reality is, I don't eat them before the race and rarely do I feel like eating them afterward. I anticipate the joys and yet am never surprised when I don't end up reaping the rewards.

That just leaves my national holidays.

Like many runners, I pay attention to my weight, and like many runners, I eat mostly what I want. When I am training, I am always hungry and can put away portions more appropriate for a teenaged football player. When I am not training, I tend not to have much of an appetite. In recent years, overwhelmed with work, I have surprised myself by becoming one of those people who forget to eat lunch. It always irritated and annoyed me when people said they forgot to eat lunch. I didn't believe them. And yet, here I am.

I do not have a calculus about how much I need to run in order to be able to eat. Instead I think about eating enough to be able to run the way I want to. I do not believe that being skinnier will make me faster. I am plenty skinny as it is. After years of battle, my body and I have come to a kind of accord, a truce. I fuel it and it performs. Sometimes I no longer even think of it as "it," but as me. This is when I know that running has done good things not just for my body.

On the Road

22

I hated you on sight.

That's perhaps too strong. But you did provoke in me a potent reaction. Like a dog whose hackles rise involuntarily, I felt my lip curl when I spotted you at baggage claim. Not a typical response from me when confronted with a lean, fit man; I don't know why I reacted to you the way I did. It was physical, chemical, unbidden.

Granted, I was tired and cranky from flying—Missoula to Minneapolis to New York to London to Delhi is a lot of hours on a lot of airplanes. And, it's true, I was anxious about the race—100 miles in five days may not seem like a lot to my friends who run that distance in less than twenty-four hours, or to you, but to me, it was daunting. Plus I feared the enforced togetherness of being part of a group, traveling as a pack, being shepherded and herded through a part of the world I feared I wasn't going to be able to really see. So I watched you, knowing that you were likely part of my group, and I felt my lip curl.

I watched you as we—a lot of Indians and only a handful of westerners—watched bags that were not ours make their way around the carousel, and waited. I saw, even from the careful distance I kept, that on your wrist you sported a yellow Lance Armstrong rubber bracelet.

LIVESTRONG. I guessed that you were fast, that the fluidity of your movements translated into swift times at hard races. I assumed that you were arrogant, cocky. I watched you talking to people; I suspected you were bragging about what you were here to do, posturing in that classic American way.

There were the two others as well. They looked less like runners, more like horses off the track: a little long in the tooth, thicker through the middle. They were also waiting. We were each at our points, at stations of the cross, around the baggage belt. I read my book and watched furtively as you went over to talk to them. I thought your smile smug. You were smiling a lot.

The woman from the Indian tourism office who had shuttled me quickly through customs and immigration came over and brought me into your little group. We were, of course, all going to the same place, all here for the same reason: the Himalayan 100-Mile Stage Race and Mount Everest Challenge Marathon. We were all, it turned out, journalists, brought over by the Indian government to beat the drum of publicity for the race.

We chatted for a bit about our publications, and then we fell into the talk that runners talk: which races we'd done, who we knew in common. We shared a quick laugh over the silly funny way an editor we both knew signed off on his e-mail messages. It was comfortable, easy, as we were rounded up and brought to the cars waiting to take us—each individually, each in his or her own car, even though the streets of Delhi were clogged with traffic and diesel fumes at 1 a.m.—to our hotel so we could sleep for a few hours before being driven back to the airport to catch the flight to Bagdogra.

I didn't sleep. None of us did. But in the morning you, at least, were perky and bright, prowling the hotel lobby, talking with people, moving, constantly moving.

On the flight I sat alone, thankfully alone, recognizing that privacy and solitude were soon to be in short supply. You sat next to Sean from *Runner's World* South Africa. Sean talked mightily. He'd done his homework, and when I passed your seats en route to the bathroom, you stopped me, wanting to point out the tallest mountains whose names Sean effortlessly pronounced: Kanchenjunga, Lhotse, Makalu, and of course, Everest. I saw only clouds. The two of you tried to train my eyes, to get me to focus, but I saw only clouds. I am often not the most perspicacious; even the highest mountains in the world can escape my notice.

But I was beginning to notice you. Your gentle ways, your inclusiveness, your open aspect—I noticed.

At the airport we picked up two more runners, twenty-something British guys, and we all loaded onto a bus. After a couple of miles of bumpy road—dodging cars, trucks, cows, pigs, goats, and children—one of the Brits asked the driver if we could ride on the roof. He'd done this when he'd traveled before through Asia; he said it was the way to go.

We scrambled up and spent the next hour perched on the metal rack, dodging trees and electric lines. You sat in back, and occasionally, to duck under a low-hanging danger, I leaned into you. It wasn't until later, when I saw the bloody scratches on your arm, I realized that you'd been whacked.

We were a multinational group—thirty-nine runners from twelve countries, with a handful of non-running journalists. It was easy to notice the superficial, the stereotypical differences among us. Indian English takes some getting used to, everything being, as it is, stated in the declarative: "You are enjoying this nice meal, and you will be showing up on time to get in the jeep when you are finished eating in five minutes." The Poms, comfortably wearing the legacy of imperialism, have the luxury of understatement and often undercut their own assertions: "Well, running one hundred miles is rather hard on the body, isn't it?" "Isn't it?" appears as frequently as we Yanks use "you know?" The Austrians are silent and aloof; when they speak it is without humility. The singular Dane waxed melancholic, a dyspeptic Hamlet.

The pre-race briefing was like every other pre-race briefing, except for the warnings about stepping off the course on the left side and entering Nepal. India has the world's largest volunteer army, and they are actively protecting the border against Maoist insurgents. We would be running on a road that formed the border; a liminal state, running on the borderlands. This felt different.

We shared a bus ride the next day, a field trip to Darjeeling on our one free day before the start of the race. We sat next to each other on the bumpy bus and offered up bits of our lives, small stories. We waited together at the station in Darjeeling to take the "Famous Toy Train." I asked if I could skip it. No, we were a group and as a group we moved. So we waited for the train. And then we saw him, the man sitting on the ground by the tracks. He'd spread out a small cloth in front of himself, and on it was a can of saffron-colored powder. I asked what you thought it was, what he was doing there, and then you were gone—squatting in front of the man, talking to him.

I followed. He was saying unintelligible things not in English and you were nodding and smiling and saying, "Yes, yes, I see." And you seemed to, really, to see. And then he dipped his finger in the powder and touched your forehead, marking you, anointing you. The man wrapped red string around your wrist, again and again, winding it frantically, another bracelet next to your yellow band. I saw the gold flash on your finger. I hadn't noticed before. Then the man asked for money and you gave him ten rupees; you gave him what you had.

I followed. The man marked my forehead, banded my wrist. Then he presented each of us with a rock, round, a perfect orb, coated in the saffron-colored powder. The group of men standing by, idling, watching the spectacle of a pair of westerners dipping a toe into Hindi culture, told us to put the rocks away. We boarded the train with rocks in our pockets.

The holy man had given us each a certificate—he'd asked our names and then filled them in, wrote an approximation of what he'd heard.

I showed the certificate to one of our guides and asked him, please, to read it for me. It was a receipt, he said, for a contribution to a church: a dedication to Shiva and Ram. I asked about the orange rock. He said it represented the god of wind; we'd been given tokens of godspeed. An auspicious start for a race, I thought. I told you about this, and warned, jovially, that you couldn't use it in your article. It was mine.

We split up, naturally, easily. On the train back one of the coupled women asked me what I'd done with my man.

My man? I didn't have a man. Not here, not in India.

Your man, she insisted. The man you're with.

She meant you. She thought you were my man.

Later I told you this and we laughed. After that, I called you my man. You soon joined in, saying I was your girl. We were calling each other "Honey" midway through the trip.

Cut off from home and family; united by a common purpose, a shared goal; a lack of creature comforts; extreme physical exertion; the relinquishing of civilian clothing for a uniform; no autonomy over meal and bed times; small acts of rebellion against the person in power—this has got to be what boot camp is like. This is how units are formed, how friendships are forged.

The first day of the race was the hardest run I've ever done: climbing six thousand feet on cobblestones as big as your head; asking yourself how much farther these 24 miles can go up and then realizing that these are the highest mountains in the world and they can go up a long damn way; legs cramping as the temperature dropped, climbing into a cloud—at nearly twelve thousand feet it's cold—this is what we do for fun? This is what we signed on for?

We met up in the food hut—our accommodations were spare wood buildings that would make the Spartans look sybaritic—with a coal fire that radiated almost no heat. I planted myself in front of the fire and stayed there, shivering. I could not get warm. People piled clothes on me, and still I shivered.

You sat down next to me and suggested hot chocolate. I demurred then changed my mind. I held the small, warm mug in my frozen paws and drank. It helped. I settled in. The other runners milled around and complained. There was lot of complaining. There had been a lot of pooping and puking on the way to this remote hut, perched on top of a peak that gave a heart-stopping view of the mother of all mountain ranges, the Himalayas. We saw Kanchenjunga nearby, no more than 50K away, looming large and icy. By contrast Everest and its neighbors looked small.

Finally I asked about your race. You said you had to stop for bathroom breaks four times. You were not feeling well, you said, but it didn't sound like complaining. The others were whingeing and whining. You were simply stating facts.

Though it seemed impossible, the next morning we rose and prepared to run again. It was an out-and-back 20 miles, at just under twelve thousand feet. I saw you when you were on your way back—I called out to my man. I was happy to see you. You, as always, seemed happy.

That afternoon, after the race, we were back in our sleeping hut and were doing impressions of Mr. C. S. Pandey, our earnest schoolmaster of a race director. We were children, giggling maniacally. And of course, it happened—just as Sean was spouting off an Indian-accented demand that we "must not be late."

"You are very bad boys and girls," he aped as Mr. C. S. Pandey walked through the door and we could not keep it together. We laughed until our faces hurt.

Mr. C. S. Pandey declared ours the "naughty hut."

The third day of the race was earmarked as a separate event. It was the Mount Everest Challenge Marathon. I wanted to run hard on this day. I cared about this. I knew that Delores, who had soundly beaten me the last two days, was a much better hill climber than I. But I knew my strengths and knew that the course was rolling for the first half, and then offered a steep and technical descent. This is what I love: hard, tough, scary. If I could catch her on the downhill, I thought, I could beat her. I wanted to win.

It was hard and it hurt. I did catch her on the downhill, but what I didn't realize is that after 9,200 feet of total descent, the race finished uphill, through the tiny town of Siri Khola and into Rimbik. I struggled for those last few miles; I wanted to cry. I was exhausted, and worse, I was leading the race. I hate leading a race, hate the fear of not knowing how far behind the next person is. We had talked about this, you and I. You said that you liked it, that you had learned, over the years, how to run your own race, how to be confident. I do not have that kind of confidence, not when it comes to racing.

But I held her off and finished: the first woman. I crossed the line and limped into the courtyard of our new accommodations. I was tired and hurting and you were the first person I saw. You had been finished for a while and looked fresh, rested. I was happy to see you and happier still when you unlaced my shoes and gave me water and cookies. The day's run had been longer than any of us expected—only Mr. C. S. Pandey believed it was just a marathon—and we had all over-extended ourselves. We were depleted, drained. But you kept moving, always moving, congratulating other finishers, helping them as you had helped me.

Our gang from the naughty hut had been separated. Women and couples were staying down here, at the Sherpa Lodge. But the men were relegated to a place a kilometer back up the hill. Delores, my new roommate complained unceasingly, giving me more details about her gastrointestinal activities than I needed or wanted to know.

Runners whine. I know this. But at races, at most races, after we finish, we go home and complain to those who love us and must put up with us. Here, we had no else to tell it to, and so we told it to each other. Everyone wanted to narrate his or her own race; everyone seemed unaware that we each had completed the same event, that we each had our own stories. We were narcissistic and boring and unaware.

"You would not believe how bad I feel," Delores said, after I finished the race on the last day, after she had already crossed the line.

"Yes," I said, "actually, I think we all know exactly how bad you feel." It is one of the things that make us least appealing, us runners, this blinkered self-absorption.

But not you. Instead of talking about yourself, you went out and talked to others. You rubbed Mimi's shoulders and suggested Bruce soak his legs in the cold water that spilled from a pipe on the lawn. You offered Sean Advil and gave Rob your blister repair kit. You encouraged the two twenty-something Englishmen, Andy and Joe, telling them the worst was behind. You reminded them, gently, of what they'd said about the race that first day while riding on the roof of the bus: "How tough can it be?"

And you learned the stories of the people who had been serving us. We had gotten used to the colonial comforts of having unseen hands doing our bidding. You found out what these workers did for the other fifty weeks of the year when they were not carrying our belongings through the mountains, when they were not refilling our water bottles or taking down our numbers. By dint of your intense curiosity and outward glance, you sucked the marrow out of this experience. While for most of us it was a race, for you it was an exercise in discovery. You smiled and said hello to everyone—many of us did this—but you took it a step further. You asked permission before you took photographs, and you asked and asked, sincere, interested questions, never seeming obtrusive or impolite. You sought to unearth the quiet things, the genius loci.

And then it was the last night. We were back where we had started the race, in Mirik. We shared a beer; neither of us were good drinkers. The beer was huge, and we were tired, spent. We got giddy and giggly. You joked that if we drank much more, you'd have to go sit on the other side of the room from me. But we drank more and it was fine and then it was time for the awards ceremony.

We sat together, inadvertently isolated from the group—a broken chair kept us together and apart. I leaned into you to whisper funny little things and we continued to laugh, not able to stop, not able to control it. You were third man in the marathon; I was second woman in the 100-mile race, first in the marathon. When we went up to collect our awards, we cheered too loudly for each other. We were asked to make speeches. I quoted you.

We sat around for a while after dinner, while the Austrian winner smoked a pipe that filled the air with a sickening, smothering scent; it seemed an act of arrogance, perhaps unwitting. I said goodnight and went up to bed.

We hugged after breakfast, having cursorily exchanged our information, promising to keep in touch. I said maybe I'd see you at a race somewhere, some time.

I got into my jeep, wanting to avoid long good-byes with the rest of the group, wanting to get it over with. I sat and waited (more waiting, so much waiting on this trip). And then I saw you come outside and without thought, without plan, I raced out and back into your arms. One more embrace.

It lasted perhaps a few seconds too long. And then you pulled back and looked down at me—I hadn't realized until just then how much taller you are—and I saw that you were going to kiss me. Right there, in front of the jeep. In front of Mr. C. S. Pandey, who already thought us naughty boys and girls. I panicked briefly, was surprised and thrilled and you leaned in and kissed me, quietly, quickly, on the mouth. One chaste kiss, after a week of sore muscles and altitude headaches and laughing until our faces hurt. One chaste kiss, after sharing silences and sandwiches and views of the most magnificent mountains in the world. One chaste kiss. No secrets, no lies. My reaction to you was physical, chemical, unbidden.

There is no name for what we were to each other for that brief time. Our connection was not romantic or sexual. We were friendly with the others on the trip, but with each other we were different. We created our own world in that faraway place. Was it simply the recognition that we were both runners, both writers, and that we saw something of ourselves in each other? That it felt like looking in the mirror? We'd been done in by those high mountains, breathless from that thin air. We were stripped down. We had nothing to hide, nothing to prove.

Perhaps we will see each other again, maybe at a race; maybe we'll hook up for coffee if it turns out we are in the same place at the same time. Perhaps. We will embrace and smile and catch up. Perhaps I'll meet your wife; I'm sure I will like her. We will laugh a bit, reminisce. But it won't be the same. We shared this time in a time that was extraordinary; it was all in the now. No future, no past. We were present for each other, there and then, in ways that we could not be in normal, daily life. We were together in that liminal space, on the border, on the threshold of what's real.

You asked me, each day we ran, if I still had my "wind," the round saffron-colored rock proffered by the holy man. I had it in my pack, carried it with me throughout the race.

When I got home, I found it was no longer there. I'd left my wind in the Himalayas, unintentionally left it where it belonged. I hold onto the memory of it, though, as palpably as if it were here in my hand.

23

The Hospital

I'm looking at the chart on the wall showing that my mother has no white blood cells left. They've been gone for three days now. I'm at her bedside, where I've been twelve hours a day, every day, in a hospital in a city that is not ours.

To treat her multiple myeloma, a cancer of the blood, her doctors have given my mother a massive dose of chemotherapy that wiped out her body's ability to defend itself. A few months before, they had stimulated growth of her stem cells and then harvested them, putting them on ice for the months it took to get the disease under control. A couple of weeks ago she was deemed strong enough to withstand this new assault on her fragile self. They eliminated her immune system and gave her back her stem cells, protean soldiers who come in, see what needs to be done, then set about doing it.

Her body has reacted as expected. She has felt increasingly fatigued, developed painful sores in her mouth and throat, and then, last night, spiked a fever.

In medicine, bad things often happen at night, when the experienced attending docs are home watching TV or sleeping. Those left minding the store are residents—people who have been doctors from fifteen minutes to a couple of years, who rotate through various services, becoming on-call experts for a few months at a time.

A long time ago when I lived with Andrew, I overheard many late night phone calls from flummoxed residents needing help and advice. Andrew always thanked them for calling, and usually he told them that their assessments were correct. But I've also heard stories of fatal screw-ups and understand that medicine is as much of an art as it is a science. Often what a physician has to go on is a good gut—the experience of having seen a lot of patients, having lived with the vicissitudes of a particular disease.

The resident on call came in. He looked like he was about twelve. He asked my mother a couple of questions about the reaction to penicillin she'd had when she was a kid. He decided it was more likely an intolerance than a true allergy and said he was going to give her a drug in the same class.

On my friendliest days, I am a pit bull. Around my sick mother, I make Harpies look seductive. I could not let this go. "Why give her something that may cause a bad reaction? Why risk it?" I whipped out my cell phone and called Andrew. He said the line about intolerance versus allergy was a classic resident stance. "But," he said, "why risk it? There are plenty of other antibiotics. What about cipro?"

I said to the resident, "What about cipro?"

We squared off. In my corner there's me, exhausted, depleted, and anxious, but having, on my cell phone, the director of a Duke clinic telling me to tell the resident to call his attending. In his corner, weighing in at maybe 180 on a five-and-a-half-foot frame is a fresh-faced guy with a ready smile who's working overnight shifts and learning to be a doctor.

He said he'd check with the pharmacist.

Then we started talking. Or rather, I started grilling him. I found out he'd gone to medical school near where I used to live. A couple of quick jabs about basketball, then he allowed that he'd had a lot of time between college and med school. I asked what he'd done. He said he'd been a professional track athlete and then a middle school history teacher.

"Which events?"

"Mile and 5000 meters."

"PRS?"

Close to four minutes flat for the mile; 14:21 in the 5K, when, he said, he had mono.

"Why didn't you run a faster 5K when you were healthy?" (Pit bull, I know.) He'd ruptured discs in his back that ended his career and kept him from the Olympic Trials in 1996. He took off eleven months, gained sixty pounds, and missed his window.

He left the room. I calmed down. My mother was getting sleepy again.

Then the former track star in a long white coat popped into the room and asked to see me. He sat me down at a computer and showed me protocols the doctors had written; he explained what everything meant with the patience and gentleness of a parent. "We'll give her cipro," he said.

We sat side by side and realized we had friends in common, having lived in the same place at the same time. He'd run against my buddies, and beaten all of them. Because he stayed on the track, I didn't recognize his name. But I recognized something in him.

I asked, three times, if it bugged him that he'd never broken four minutes. He just smiled and said no. I pushed, wanting to know what had motivated him.

"Running was something I knew I could do," he said. He told me that he had grown up here, in upstate New York, and was the first of his five siblings to go to college. Same for his wife, who he'd been with for twenty years. He talked about her with the twinkle and blush you see in the recently smitten.

"No one thought I could make it to college," he said. "No one thought I could be a track athlete. Or go to medical school. But I knew I could. I knew I could."

When the resident had first come into my mother's room, I noticed he'd touched her lightly as he spoke. Doctors can diagnose many ailments without ever doing a physical examination. But there is something powerful about touch; when we are weak, we need connection. Good docs know this.

That night, as my mother's fever began to wane, I knew that her doctor had touched me as well. It's not that I need my mother's caregivers to be runners, to know the things I know, to share a passion. But that night, when I was scared and confused, it sure didn't hurt.

Pacing

24

Eos, the Greek goddess of dawn, took a human lover, Tithonus. She asked mighty Zeus to grant him immortality, ensuring herself an everlasting plaything. He did. But Eos forgot to ask Zeus to also grant her tender vittle agelessness. So poor Tithonus got older and older, smaller and smaller, and became less and less appealing. Eventually Tithonus turned into a cricket.

Most of us want to keep running for our entire mortal lives. But age is a greater foe than the fiercest of the Greek gods. While I'm not yet nearing insectitude, I realize that if I want to keep enjoying my running, I have to look for different kinds of challenges. Many of my runner friends have been turning to triathlons to spice up their athletic lives. I would do that, except for the swimming and biking parts. Doing longer races means you don't have to run as fast, and that's always nice. But there's something else I've found that has given me more pleasure, and more meaning, than any other running-related activity.

I was fortunate to be tapped for the Clif Bar Pace Team. We are a pack of two dozen people, from various and diverse backgrounds, who carry wooden dowels with balloons tied to them (yes, there must be a better way, but one has come up with it yet) and lead groups at marathons. We run times ranging from 3:10 to 5:30. We meet six to eight times a year to work together at the marathon expo booth, have meals, and get updates on each other's lives, work, and families. Sharon can always be counted on to have whatever anyone has forgotten; Scott bakes chocolate chip and snickerdoodle cookies for the group; when Michelle and I room together, we stay up too late talking. It's fun to be part of a team.

But the real fun is the pacing. At the expo, we sign people up and give instructions on where to find us on race morning. We answer questions—about training, marathoning, nutrition, and hydration. We caution first-timers about picking a reasonable goal. We introduce ourselves and say we look forward to running with them. And we do.

We are volunteers. We give up our time and energy—for a handful of Clif Bars, uniforms and shoes, and a fancy watch—to pace at about thirty minutes slower than our typical marathon times. We do not get paid, though our expenses to the races are covered. We are mostly loud, extroverted, enthusiastic people who, though we each have our own running goals, love to help other people meet theirs.

We are allowed to be plus or minus two minutes at the halfway point, and must finish no more than two minutes fast at the end. On our balloons we draw happy faces, write our names, and advertise our finishing times. That's what we've committed to run, and that's what we run, regardless of what happens in the group. All of my teammates are able to finish within seconds of their projected time.

We line up before the race under big, bright signs. We gather around us our groups. Since marathons usually begin when the temperature is cool, I'm often cold at the start, so I've made a practice of going to thrift stores to outfit myself with pre-race sweatpants and sweatshirts that I can leave behind. Sometimes I even buy coats. I look like a bag lady and people often come to my sign and ask where the pacer is. "I'm the pacer," I tell them, and they look at me skeptically. Just before the start, I strip down to my Clif Bar Pacer uniform—singlet and shorts—and I give my usual pep talk.

I tell them that I take it personally if they do not finish with me; it hurts my feelings. I expect them to be with me through the half, but want them to be with me at the end. It makes me feel good to help others achieve their goals; that's why I do this. Please remember, I implore, this is not about you—it's all about me. I tell them that we will run even splits, keeping as close to the goal pace as possible. The miles at the start can be tricky—often it's crowded and hard to get on track. But then I will click into the pace and hold it for the rest of the race. All they need to do is follow me and my balloons.

Generally we start off with hordes of people around us. Since we tend to pace at big marathons, often, at the half, we still have big groups. Inevitably, at mile 20 or so, things begin to thin out. At the Los Angeles Marathon, a big guy who was running right near me said, as I was rhapsodizing about the joys of In-N-Out Burgers, that if I got him to the finish in four hours, he would get me a big bag of them. I said that I would be there; he just had to stick with me. I ended up buying my own burger.

As the race goes on, the numbers dwindle. I call out: "Do I still have my group?" They answer, those who are left, but after 17 or 18 miles, their voices are weak. When we hit the twenties, they are mostly silent. I try to keep up a patter. While in the beginning I may have told jokes, later in the race I try to tell stories. I tell them about my first pacing experience, meeting Liz at the New York Marathon and how she tracked me down to thank me. I tell them about all the people who have followed me to a Boston qualifying time. I lie to them for miles: "You're looking good." "You're doing great." "You're going to make it."

Sometimes people who have started out more conservatively will join me later in the race. At around mile 18 in L.A., I met up with two girls. They told me we'd be running past their houses in a few miles, and then, soon after that, The Marlborough School, where they were juniors.

I asked them about their college applications and when they answered, I told them that this was their lucky day: I am high-priced college admissions consultant. If they stuck with me, they could get hundreds of dollars of free counseling. We talked about SATs, recommendations, and which topics to avoid for the essay. At mile 23, I told Christina—whose longest run had been 8 miles—to go ahead; we were slowing her down. Celia finished with me, in 3:58, ready to apply to Harvard.

Frequently, though, I run the last few miles alone. I carry my balloons, keeping the same pace I have run all morning through the finish line. I know there are people following me who are using my balloons as a beacon, that I am pulling them with me, even if they have fallen behind. It used to upset me that I could not get my whole group all the way to the finish in their goal time. Then a friend reminded me that I can't do the running for them, can't do their training. All I can do is keep the pace and be encouraging. After I cross the line, I wait and cheer for them as they come in. Sweating, sometimes crying, they embrace and thank me.

Each pacer has an arsenal of stories about why he or she loves to pace. One of my favorites is from Scott, the cookie-maker. One guy, he said, had been with the group for most of the race but had fallen back a bit the last few miles. After Scott crossed the finish line, he congratulated the runners in his group, and then waited around, as we all do, to congratulate the runners who had fallen off the pace. He saw the guy cross the line and went to shake his hand. The guy said, "That is not going to do it," and he gave Scott a big bear hug and planted a kiss on his cheek. "I don't remember his name," Scott says, "but I will never forget his face."

I have had to adjust my own running goals. It is clear that my speedy times are behind me. Even my respectable times are getting to be a distant memory. It would bother me more, this inevitable decline, I think, if it weren't for pacing. Students who are forced to do community service often learn that it's more satisfying to help others than it is to indulge yourself. Being a pacer has opened up my running world. From my first unofficial pacing duties—Ralph at Western States, Liz in New York—I saw the possibilities of how rewarding this job could be.

It is, for now, a way to sustain me as a runner, though it also, at times, feels like a job. I have to be marathon-ready all year. I bridle at having to wear a uniform—I prize my individual style—but, like everyone, I enjoy getting free stuff. I don't enjoy being bossed around and assigned tasks, but some of those tasks—like hanging out at a marathon expo and talking to runners, some of whom I've met at other races—are fun.

And the pay is great: a thank you and a kiss, I've come to think, are much more compelling than a PR or a Shiny Metal Object.

25

The Break Up

It is ballast. Too heavy. I can't carry this around with me, can't bear the load.

I don't want to go out for a run. Easier pull the shades on the feelings, curl up and let the pillow soak with escaped tears. I don't want to be in the sun, on the trail, not now, not today.

But I am dragging on shorts, taking a dirty shirt out of the laundry basket, drawing over my head the rankness of my own self. Why not encircle myself in the stink? I'm heading out the door.

Into this harsh sun. Squinty eyes behind sunglasses. Keep them covered. Make it hurt. Make this physical. Take it out on the body. Exorcize it.

Early on he said, "I didn't think I was your type."

He was right, but still, I asked why.

"Not a skinny runner guy," he said.

No. And all the other things he was not.

He rode his bike while I ran. He didn't care about going fast or far, just liked the company. We'd spent the morning talking about books. He made breakfast for me in my house; he cooked with a pan I didn't know I had. He created a meal out of things that would never have come together if I had been alone.

We talked about Ben Franklin. He told me about Franklin's reading group, the Junto, where people from diverse backgrounds came together each Friday night and brought to the table things they had found interesting, and shared them for the benefit of all. They met for mutual improvement and pledged to respect each other, regardless of religion; they agreed to seek truth.

He said it sounded like a writing workshop, or some ideal version of one.

I thought, but did not say, that it sounded like my weekly running group.

In the afternoon we started the talk that would bring us to this point. If we're not going forward, moving toward something, do we stop? Even if we care about each other, can we be together? We had some things in common, but were they the right things? I was, he grumbled, always shivering, not comfortable living in the outdoors. We had talked about my going on a river trip with him and some friends. We both knew I wouldn't have liked it. You would have been cold, he said. You wouldn't have liked the wet, he said. For him it has been a perfect week.

I said it didn't matter that he didn't run. Was this true? Or was it that I wanted it to be true? I had started running because I didn't want to be left behind. Was I afraid that he wasn't going to be able to keep up? Men my own age often complain that I have too much energy, that I make them feel old and tired. We were born a year apart, me first. He seemed a lot older.

The guy I dated before him was a runner. That guy had been my type: a sub-three hour marathoner with a fancy academic pedigree who taught at an Ivy League university. A guy who showered twice a day and never washed off the ambition. A guy, runner-thin, who, when I first undressed in front of him, looked at me—my body hard and toned from running, but far from perfect, the body of a forty-five-year-old woman—and said: "I guess I have to start going to the gym." He mentioned his age so often that I couldn't forget it—he was a handful of years older than me—and I began to think of him as old. That he was a runner didn't seem to help.

"You're always cold," he said. It's true. And when I'm cold, I have a bad habit of announcing it to the world. I know I should try to keep quiet, but I cannot handle being both quiet and cold. He was quick to try to warm me, to hold me close in ursine embrace, to offer warmer layers. His clothes smelled of wood smoke and work, even when they were new and laundered. He smelled too much of the earth for me; lived too close to it. I prefer a layer of deodorant to cloak our humanity.

We hiked together a few times, day hikes up mountains and down. He ambled, stopping to look at the stumps of trees that had been logged out a hundred years before, picked up a cone from a Doug fir and pointed out the way it looked like a bunch of mouse butts, back haunches and tails. I kissed him for that.

But I was always waiting ahead, wishing I was running, covering more ground. Seeing more, I'd say, even though I knew that wasn't right. He named the lupine and the cottonwoods and spotted the small-eared owl. He pulled the tick out of my hair. He noticed. I covered ground.

It would have been easier, I told him, if we could have done this on a run, thrown out these hard things without having to watch them land on each other's faces.

"Maybe," he said. "But I don't run."

I cannot keep still.

It is not true that if a shark stops moving he will die. That is an urban legend. But it is an irresistible metaphor.

I do not want to be in a relationship with him. We are not a good fit. His sentences are too loose, his gait too slow, his body malodorous and too comfortably upholstered. I cannot imagine ever being able to live with him.

We were friends first, and will be again. Soon, probably. I know this. We both have good histories of keeping people in our lives, after the romance has played out.

I told him what Dave, an old ex-boyfriend, had said to me last summer, when we were at a bar—a night of close friends who, a long time ago, had shared a bed—talking about basketball and people we both knew, asking about each other's families, him drinking too many beers, me sipping hot water with lemon.

"Why didn't it work out with us?" Dave had said, with the same near-angry look he gets when I ask about his drinking. "I really love you," he said, almost with surprise.

"It did work out," I said. "This what it looks like, sometimes, to have something work out."

I cannot stop crying. My pace has slowed and I still have 2 more miles to go. The breathing is getting in my way. Images flash, a PowerPoint in my head. A night, not so long ago—we didn't last that long—when he sat too close to me on the couch. The way he took my hand and pulled me to him. I pulled away—saying, "No, it's not right. I can't afford to lose you as a friend." And then, kissing my friend. And kissing him again.

Was I lying when I said that it didn't matter that he wasn't a runner? Was it possible that his body—whose muscles did not announce themselves with the flamboyance of those with less padding—could ever be attractive to me? Would what we shared in books and politics and mutual friends be enough? Could running be beside the point? When I jumped out of bed on Sunday mornings to meet my long run guys, it was not upsetting to him; he didn't mind that I went. But I thought about the groups of men I've run with over the years, married men whose wives were shut out of this part of their lives, this important part of their lives. Is it too much to ask? How much can you expect a partner to share?

I cannot stop crying though I know it is silly. I do not want to be sad. I want to rejoice in having tried this experiment, and more, having ended it in such a grownup way, with no angry words, with no recriminations or accusations. I should be relieved; when I was with him I found myself looking with lust and longing at the bodies of running men. It shouldn't have been like that, not if it was right.

There is no loss. It was only an idea. Farewell to an idea, then.

As I near my house I realize the lungs have relaxed. The tears have stopped. The running has helped. But as I slide off my shoes, wiggle out of my shorts, and let the water in the shower get warm, it all comes back. The miles didn't solve anything. They gave me time and space to catalog, masked tears with sweat, but nothing has changed. I still want to pull the shades, cover my head.

It is not a panacea, running, as much as I wish it were.

I cannot run away. Not from myself.

I step into the shower and begin, once again, to cry.

The Curtain Rod

26

It is a visual pun. I would not have thought to make it, being, as I've been accused more than once, "domestically disabled." But my friend Candace is a whiz at making a house feel like a home, and when I moved to a new place, she came to help feather my nest. She did lots of obvious stuff, like arrange furniture and hang pictures, but because she is an artist, she did things that would never have occurred to me. The curtain rod was one of them.

When I first started running, and racing, I collected my trophies like rare coins—keeping them safe, basking in the pride of ownership. Even cheap plastic ones, even the silly medallions from age group awards at tiny, out-of-the-way, sparsely populated races. As I raced more and won more, I always stayed around for the awards. I run for smos, I told people. Shiny Metal Objects. They don't have to be shiny, or even metal; they are markers of where I've been and what I've done. I kept every one until the collection got big enough that I needed to share it with the world.

So I created the "Shrine to Me." If you walked in the front door of my house, it was the first thing you would see: a ragtag collection of pewter plates from a half marathon in Williamsburg, Virginia; the marble-based pen stand I won at my first marathon; a Durham Bulls baseball from a 5K that ended at the stadium; a framed color Xerox, a little smudged, proclaiming me the female champion of the Gold Country Marathon; a rock etched with Rattlesnake 50K, the reminder of my winning "Best Blood"; a Christmas ornament from the "Snowflake 50K"; a bell jar from a half marathon in Parkersburg, West Virginia, that was sponsored by a scientific glass company; a ceramic Kokanee salmon from a trail half marathon; a silver plate from the Mount Everest Marathon encased in Lucite (first place) and a similar silver plate, now dark and tarnished for lack of Lucite, for the Himalayan 100-mile race (second place); a multi-colored collection of Ride and Tie belt buckles, many announcing in gaudy but real silver and gold Top Ten finishes; the gigantic trophy, with my name, the female winner of the Black Mountain Marathon, that Candace had made for me after I won the race and complained that my prize, a watercolor by a local artist, was not a real SMO. And dozens of marathon finisher's medals.

Before I moved west, I culled the collection. I had been running long enough, and winning plenty of times, that I was ready to part with the least precious of my medals; I kept only the biggest and the most rare. But I did keep all of the marathon medallions, if only because it was a way of knowing how many marathons I'd actually run.

These, Candace said, were the problem. We needed to find something to do with them.

She looked around the new house. She looked at the window. And the light went on.

There were only mini-blinds on the windows. I am not a person who has ever had curtains. Candace made a valance—one of those weird, short, window treatments that hang atop curtains—out of my medals. There were enough of them to make a thick ornamental drape. A visual pun.

The Shrine to Me. It's with a strong sense of irony, and amused self-awareness, that I look on the objects that commemorate where

I've been and what I've done. I've been running for more than fifteen years now. It feels like I've been a runner my whole life.

A couple of years ago I got one of those out-of-the-blue, blast-from-the-past e-mails from a guy I'd known in high school. We'd not been friends, not really. He'd hung out with the smart kids. He was kind of a geek. It was before I appreciated that the geeks will inherit the earth. But I sat behind him in typing class and was impressed by how readily he grasped concepts in physics. He'd been messing around on the computer, he said, and decided to track me down. A quick Google search confirmed things that did not surprise him: that I wrote, that I taught. (In truth, these things surprised me, but we are often not the best predictors of our own lives.) What shocked him was that I was a runner. And not only a runner, an ultramarathoner. That, he said, he would not have expected.

Nor would I. Val and Andrew will occasionally allow themselves a giggle when they think back to our trip to the Outer Banks, staying at the Ancient Marnier, my dismissal of their desire to run and the pronouncement that lying on the deck with novel and Oreos close at hand was surely the reasonable choice.

My family has finally learned not to ask me, after I race, the dreaded question: "Did you win?" My mother, while she still worries about how frequently I fall during trail races, seems to take my doing a marathon or an ultra in stride. Just as she has gotten used to my having a rat, or a pig, as a pet. My brother has woken at ungodly hours to drive me to races, collected what's left of me afterward, and always feeds me exactly what I want both before and after. During visits they expect me to leave for an hour or longer each day to go for a run. If I don't go, they ask why not.

I used to spend a lot of time looking at my books. I'd cast a gaze over the spines and settle on old friends, dearly beloveds, and those I'd not yet had the time to read but reminded myself that I wanted to. I'd remember where I was when I'd read each one, where I'd lived, with whom, what I'd been doing. My books were a way of marking time and place.

I still do that with my books. But I also do it with the Shrine to Me. I look at my living room window and see the curtain of medals, stamped with dates and places, each like a bite of Proust's muffin, each able to provoke the remembrance of things past, and I think about the space on the rod that's still left to be filled.

Getting to the Finish

It happened again. Trotting along in a marathon, not working hard, a little bored, I started talking to a woman going my pace and exerting herself no more nor less than I. We did the geographical check-in—she was from Canada. We did the number of marathons—she'd done forty-eight to my forty-something. She looked at me, and then asked my name.

"Ah," she said. "I've read you."

Nothing gives me a greater boost than to be recognized by my byline. It's happened frequently enough that I shouldn't be surprised, yet each time I meet a reader, and especially those who pay close attention and can quote me back to me, or remind me of thoughts I'd forgotten I'd had, I feel like I could run faster and farther than I'd believed possible just moments before.

It's one thing to put yourself on the page from the comfort of home—sometimes even from bed—but somehow, when you're writing, you don't think about being read. You imagine, perhaps, some ideal reader whom you are trying to impress, to wow, but it's hard to think of your writing as a product, out there in the world. But off it goes, and then all these people come into your life because they liked what you had to say and how you said it. It keeps me going to races, and keeps me going at them.

What often gets me through that last quarter of a mile in a marathon is remembering the things I have heard from readers during races—the nice comments, the recognition that they know me in some way. As I struggle to the finish, I can get a burst by recalling an "I love your writing," even if it was said years ago at another race.

Some people become runners on their own. As this book shows, I didn't. A posse of people have gotten me to the starting line. I cannot thank them enough: my first coach, Peter Klopfer, put me on the right track; his wife, Martha, continues to inspire me. Audrey Baldessari was kind enough to slow her pace to run with me. Sarah Flanagan and Valerie Chang were girls who ran when we were girls, and are still my friends, now that we are women. My Durham running peeps, including (but surely, unforgivably, forgetting others) Owen Astrachan, Jeff Forbes, Walter Rogan, Jim Claebusch, Carolyn Huettel, Ole Holsti, Gordon Keeler, Cathy Wides, Scott Schoedler, Stephen Frasier, Steve Leopard, Roger Sutton, Ralph Tuttle, Chris Shields, Guido Ferrari, Denise Larson. The Missoula crowd: Jeff Bookwalter, Dean McGovern, Jason Lathrop, Ashley Parkinson, Jeff Crouch, Joe Campana, Eric Digby, Mo Hartman, Kevin Twidwell, Chuck Hansberry and my Missoula family, David, Becky, Sage and Nadine Brooks. The people I've met at races: Nikki Kimball, Don Demetriades, Charlie Charman, Mo Livermore, David Horton, Eric Davis, Sophie Spiedel, Dan Lehmann, Katie Stettler, Lorrie Tilly, Becky Harmon, Boris Dzikovski, Diane Sherrer, and Alan and Nate Lockett.

I'm grateful to my Ride and Tie partners over the years: Mary Tiscornia, Elaine Ruprecht, "Irish" Mike Whelen, Jeannie, Laura, Audrey, Cimarron, Slick (an asshole at the start), and that little sports car of a horse, Albi, and to all the members of the Ride and Tie family for making me feel at home right from the beginning.

Mike Pastore was at mile 60 of the Umstead 100 when he saw me, recognized me, and told me that he'd read everything I'd written. I ran with him for a few miles, and he told me that when he'd read my piece about pacing Ralph at Western States, he'd said to his wife that he wished he could find a pacer like me when he ran Western. I'll pace you, I said, and I did. And then I did it again. And hope to again and again.

My Clif BarPace teammates have been fabulous—we see each other at races all over the country and it is usually a joyful reunion. Our fearless leaders, Darris and Starshine Blackford keep us in line. I adore them all, but I'm especially grateful to Sharon McNary and Scott Stocker, for always having everything I need but have forgotten, and to Michelle Laroche for being such a good roommate that we never get enough sleep.

I am grateful to the North Carolina School of Science and Math 2003 cross-country team, as well as to the brave students in my freshman English section of the University of Montana's Davidson Honors College who came with me to a local 10K. The creative writing majors at Eastern Washington University who took my course on writing about sports proved invaluable as readers: Mikita Hellie, smart, scrappy, who will someday be a sportswriter; Erica Chang, who is learning to be a big girl; Ivory Freeman, a beautiful writer, a smart reader, and an excellent rat sitter; and Robin Hansen, who had the nerve to learn too well and remind me what I needed to do to write this book.

I'm lucky to have had astute readers who aren't runners: Judy Blunt saw many of these pieces in a graduate workshop; she was a mentor and is now a good friend. Nancy Cook, in our writing group of two, helped me to figure out what this book is about and how to make it better. Steve Reinertsen read an early draft and gave helpful comments. From him I know that avocados are fruit, not vegetables. They are still, however, disgusting.

I have been fortunate to work with a number of excellent editors. Don Allison published one of the first pieces I ever wrote on running on his Coolrunning.com Web site, and then many of my race reports in *Ultrarunning*. *Marathon&Beyond*'s Rich Benyo has taken more words from me than most writers could ever hope for, and sends e-mails and letters that always make me smile. Karen Winkler, at the *Chronicle of Higher Education*, let me do a piece on running for that esteemed and lofty publication.

My peeps at *Running Times* have been the best—combining professionalism and warmth. My first editorial meeting with Jonathan Beverly was a 10-mile run on Manhattan's West Side to the little red lighthouse under the great gray bridge. We always have about fourteen different conversations going, and even when we disagree, I learn from him. Jim Gerweck knows everything about running. And he's just a plain old good guy. Jane Hoffman and Alicia O'Neill, both marathoners and fellow big-boobed running bra testers, helped out at the final hour by reading the manuscript and providing useful feedback.

Candace Karu started off as a colleague from *Running Times* and is now someone on whom I depend for almost everything. We have often talked on the phone for longer than it takes either of us to run a marathon. She is part of my family, as are the REBS, the Fraternal Brotherhood of Rachel's Ex-boyfriends. Without Andrew Krystal I would never have become a runner. Or, for that matter, a writer. Without Mike Bergmann, I would not be able to survive in the world.

My agent, Susan Arellano, ends up making about seven cents an hour working on my books. She reads everything I write and replies with a rapidity and incisiveness that makes my head spin. Finding a good agent is an essential part of being a happy author. I lucked out.

My mother, the cutest, most wonderful, most loved mother in the whole wide world, has shown throughout her long illness a strength and fortitude that inspires and awes me; often during races I think about how tough my cute little mother has been and it gets me through. My brother has made a family for himself. He loves his wife, Allyn, and their daughter, Eva, with a fierce tenderness. And he loves me, and supports me, in ways huge and trivial (though his cooking is by no means trivial). I'm sure I don't tell him enough how much I respect, admire, and love him.

At the University of Nebraska Press, Ladette Randolph, publisher of many of my friends, encouraged this project from the beginning and put me in touch with Rob Taylor, who has been stalwart in his support. I was fortunate to have a fellow runner, Joeth Zucco, copyedit the manuscript and Ashley Muehlbauer design the book. Dave Mankin, my *fautor meus*, the northeastern outpost of the REBS, came, as usual, to my rescue at the very end of this process. Katerina Stanton gave the manuscript a final, rigorous, philological read, catching many of my mistakes and making good and useful suggestions. Like the best editors, coaches, and pacers, Kat saw where I was trying to go, and helped me get there.

Much of my writing, and all of my reading, is done with a small vermin perched on my shoulder or lap. Iris is my inspiration, my delight, my companion. I thought that having a rat would be less of an emotional undertaking than getting another dog. Boy was I wrong—so happily wrong. I am in love with someone the size of a pickling cucumber.

Finally, thanks here to all my readers. And most especially, to those who have come out to me and announced themselves as such. I look forward to seeing you on the roads, on the trails, and at the races.

Source Acknowledgments

A portion of chapter 8, "Ride and Ties," was published as "A Horse Called Slick," in *Marathon&Beyond* (July/August 2004).

Chapter 9, "Weekend Mornings," was published in a slightly different form in *Running Times* (October 2007).

Chapter 11, "Speed Goggles," was originally published in *Running Times* (March, 2007).

A slightly different version of chapter 14, "Becoming a Marathoner" was originally published as "My Most Unforgettable Marathon and What I Learned From It" in *Marathon&Beyond*, (January/February 2004).

Part of chapter 15, "Racing," was originally published in *Running Times* (January/February 2006).

Chapter 16, "The Western State," was originally published as "Easing the Loneliness of the Long Distance Runner" in *Marathon&Beyond* (June/July 2003).

Part of chapter 18, "Ultras," was originally published in *Marathon & Beyond* (May/June 2008).

A slightly different version of chapter 22, "On the Road," was published in *Marathon&Beyond* (September/October 2005).

Chapter 23, "The Hospital," was originally published as "Runners When and Where You Need Them," in *Running Times* (May 2007).

Chapter 24, "Pacing," was originally published in slightly different form as "Your Pace or Mine," in *Running Times* (November 2006).